CRIMINAL JUSTICE

Evidence

CRIMINAL JUSTICE

Crime and Criminals

Crime Fighting and Crime Prevention

Evidence

The Law

Prison and the Penal System

Trials and the Courts

CRIMINAL JUSTICE

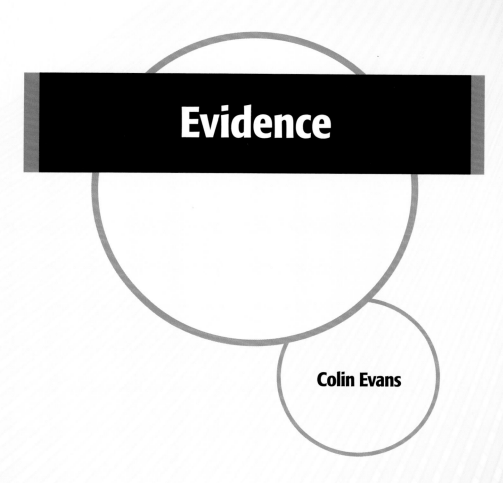

Evidence

Colin Evans

CHELSEA HOUSE
PUBLISHERS
An imprint of Infobase Publishing

CRIMINAL JUSTICE: Evidence

Chelsea House
An imprint of Infobase Publishing
132 West 31st Street
New York NY 10001

Library of Congress Cataloging-in-Publication Data
Evans, Colin, 1948-
Evidence / Colin Evans.
p. cm. — (Criminal justice)
Includes bibliographical references and index.
ISBN-13: 978-1-60413-615-9 (hardcover : alk. paper)
ISBN-10: 1-60413-615-4 (hardcover : alk. paper) 1. Evidence, Criminal.
2. Criminal investigation. I. Title.
HV8073.E9254 2010
363.25'6—dc22
2009043848

Chelsea House books are available at special discounts when purchased in bulk quantities for businesses, associations, institutions, or sales promotions. Please call our Special Sales Department in New York at (212) 967-8800 or (800) 322-8755.

You can find Chelsea House on the World Wide Web at http://www.chelseahouse.com

Text design by Erika K. Arroyo
Cover design by Keith Trego
Composition by EJB Publishing Services
Cover printed by Bang Printing, Brainerd, MN
Book printed and bound by Bang Printing, Brainerd, MN
Date printed: April 2010

Printed in the United States of America

10 9 8 7 6 5 4 3 2 1

This book is printed on acid-free paper.

All links and Web addresses were checked and verified to be correct at the time of publication. Because of the dynamic nature of the Web, some addresses and links may have changed since publication and may no longer be valid.

Contents

Introduction

Whenever a crime is committed, investigators search for evidence that they hope will lead to the perpetrator. This evidence can take many forms. It might be the testimony of an eyewitness, a fragment of **DNA** or a fingerprint, a fiber, some documents, or perhaps even a confession. Whatever form it takes, evidence falls into one of two categories; it is either direct or circumstantial. Although the law recognizes no distinction between direct and circumstantial evidence—in court each is accorded the same weight—there is an important difference between them. This can best be explained by giving an example.

If a witness testifies that he saw a defendant deliberately and without provocation, fire a bullet into the body of a person who then died, then this constitutes direct evidence of murder (providing, of course, that the witness is telling the truth.) On the other hand, if the witness testifies that he heard a shot and that when he arrived on the scene seconds later he saw the defendant standing over the corpse with a gun in his hand, this is circumstantial evidence because other possibilities then exist. For instance, the person holding the gun might have been shooting at the escaping killer; or he might have been an innocent bystander who just happened to pick up the gun after the killer had dropped it and fled. This is what makes circumstantial evidence so tricky and has led to the common misconception that someone cannot be convicted on circumstantial evidence alone. Nothing could be further from the truth; in fact, the majority of convictions are based on circumstantial evidence. This is because most criminals tend to commit their crimes away from the prying eyes of witnesses and not all are obliging enough to leave evidence such as a fingerprint or DNA traces in their wake, which although not direct evidence *per se*, are very strong indicators of someone's presence at a crime scene.

With that important clarification out of the way, it is necessary to next look at how evidence is gathered. The most important aspect of any investigation is crime scene integrity. It is absolutely vital. The old days of cigarette-smoking detectives blundering clumsily about a murdered

THE EYEWITNESS CONTROVERSY

Probably the oldest form of evidence known to mankind is the eyewitness. On the face of it, what could be more damning than someone testifying that "I saw the defendant shoot the victim"? The answer is: quite a lot. Eyewitness identification of strangers—especially in traumatic circumstances, such as witnessing or being the victim of a violent crime—is notoriously unreliable. In 1989 James Calvin Tillman was convicted of raping and robbing a woman in Hartford, Connecticut. The only substantive evidence against him was the eyewitness testimony of the victim. Tillman swore he was innocent. But without any fresh evidence to support that claim, no appeal court would quash the verdict. Eventually his case came to the attention of the Innocence Project,[1] an organization that seeks to overturn wrongful convictions. Mostly it operates by subjecting old evidence samples to the latest advances in DNA technology. Tillman proved to be one of its greatest triumphs. In 2006, after spending 18 years behind bars, Tillman was finally exonerated after DNA testing definitively excluded him as the source of trace evidence found on the victim's body. His ordeal is only one of hundreds of horror stories based on mistaken eyewitness testimony and highlights the difficulties attached to this type of evidence. Some courts, but not all, now direct juries on the problems associated with this kind of testimony.

Mistaken eyewitness testimony is far from being a modern problem. In 1858 an Illinois man named William "Duff" body are long gone. A modern crime scene has become an extension of the forensic laboratory, and this demands that it is processed in a thoroughly scientific manner. First, the area is secured. Then it is videoed. Next comes still photography. No matter how illuminating a moving record of the crime scene might be, the high-quality still image is unbeatable when it comes to recording evidence in minute detail. At one time a dozen photographs were considered sufficient to document a crime scene; nowadays, as many as 200 images are recorded.

Armstrong stood trial, accused of murdering James Metzker on the night of August 29, 1857. The prosecution's case rested on the testimony of its key witness, Charles Allen, who said that, on the night of the murder, he distinctly saw Armstrong strike Metzker with a sling-shot. Although he had been 150 feet away at the time of the murderous attack—around 11:00 P.M.—Allen claimed that he had been able to see the incident quite clearly because there was a full moon.

This sounded devastating, and few gave Armstrong much chance of avoiding the gallows, until his counsel began to question Allen. He was particularly interested in the position of the full moon at the time of the attack. An exasperated Allen was obliged to repeat a dozen or so times that it had been directly overhead. Eventually Armstrong's counsel asked the court's permission to introduce an almanac into evidence. Judge James Harriot granted the request. The almanac, with its astronomical tables, showed that not only was there not a full moon on the night in question, but that there had been *no moon at all!* Allen slunk from the witness stand, exposed as a perjurer. (Some suspected that he was the real killer.) The jury quickly decided that Armstrong was innocent and he was set free. Armstrong's lawyer—an old friend of the accused who had done the case *pro bono*—moved on to bigger and better things. Just three years later he was President of the United States. High office, indeed, but Abraham Lincoln always regarded the Armstrong acquittal as the pinnacle of his legal career.

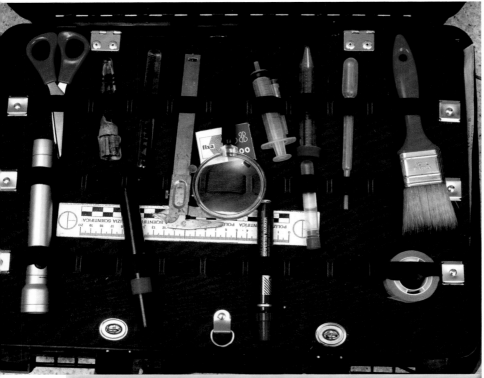

This crime-scene investigation kit contains the tools used to find, collect, and record evidence. Tools include a flashlight, marker pens, a ruler, calipers, and scissors. The sticky tape, syringe, and pipette are used to collect hair, fibers, and liquids. *Mauro Fermariello/Photo Researchers, Inc.*

After this, criminalists—trained specialists, rather than detectives—move in. It is their job to comb every square inch of the crime scene in a search for clues. Any trace evidence they discover—a fiber or a fragment of hair—is bagged and labeled. That item is then dispatched to the crime lab for analysis. To satisfy the courts and the needs of justice, every step of its journey has to be documented in scrupulous detail. This is called the chain of custody, and it is absolutely crucial to the judicial process. Any hint of misconduct or negligence on the part of the investigators can have calamitous results, perhaps even leading to an item of evidence being ruled inadmissible by the courts.

The chain of custody protocol extends far beyond the crime scene. It governs not only how evidence is gathered, but also what happens to that evidence afterward. Transporting samples from the crime scene to the lab and then to the court in a satisfactory manner requires a transparent and, above all, properly documented paper trail. The protocol covers the seizure, custody, control, transfer, analysis, and disposition of all kinds of physical and electronic evidence. Each person—or link—in the chain must document his or her exposure to that particular item of evidence—how long it was in his or her possession, for instance—and what happened next to that item. These details are recorded on a chain of custody card that provides a chronological description of who handled what and when.

Assuming that the various items of evidence from a crime scene have been processed in a correct and proper manner, one absolutely crucial question remains to be asked—what exactly is evidence? In law, evidence basically refers to any material item or assertion of fact that may be submitted to a court, in order to aid that court in its search to discover whether the defendant is guilty as charged or innocent. This is not always as clear-cut as it sounds. First and foremost, the evidence has to be relevant and admissible. This will generally be decided by the presiding judge, who can call on centuries of legal precedent in reaching his or her decision. Typical questions that the judge will ask are: Is this item of evidence relevant to the case? Was the search warrant that led to the discovery of this evidence properly authorized? Was the defendant apprised of his or her rights before making any kind of statement about this evidence? Is there any evidence of coercion in the obtaining of a confession? All these questions and more need to be answered to the judge's satisfaction before an item of evidence may be admitted into testimony. But there is another category of evidence, and this is where the lines become far more blurred.

SCIENCE TAKES A HAND

The explosion of forensic science at the beginning of the 20th century raised the evidence admissibility bar by several notches. There were no legal precedents, for example, for **chromatographs** and comparison

Evidence labels are sealed with wax; each time the seals are broken, the reason for doing so must be recorded and new seals affixed. This prevents tampering and preserves the chain of custody. *Patrick Landmann/Photo Researchers, Inc.*

microscopes; these were brand new tools in the fight against crime, and the courts had to find a way of assessing their acceptability. The answer came in a landmark case known as *Frye v. United States 293 F. 1013 (D.C. Cir. 1923)*.

The *Frye* decision established that, for evidence of a technical nature to be admissible, it had to be generally accepted by the scientific community, and that this acceptance needed to be grounded in experimentation bolstered by rigorous peer review (this is where other scientists study the methodology of the experiments, the data gathered, and agree that it conforms with accepted scientific principles.) And for 70 years Frye ruled the roost. But on March 30, 1993, the United State Supreme Court heard the suit of a family that had sued Merrell Dow Pharmaceuticals over its drug Bendectin. The Dauberts claimed that their son, Jason, had suffered birth defects because Mrs. Daubert had taken Bendectin during pregnancy. Merrell Dow moved for summary judgment

THE FRYE DECISION

One of the most significant cases in American jurisprudence arose out of a shooting incident on the night of November 27, 1920, when a wealthy doctor, Robert W. Brown, was shot and killed at his home in Washington, D.C. A lull came over the investigation until the following August, when Secret Service agents arrested a 24-year-old local man named James A. Frye on a charge of forging a Treasury check. Acting on a tip-off, detectives asked to interview Frye. Under their grilling, Frye allegedly admitted having killed Brown, providing details of the incident that only the culprit would know, and revealing where the murder weapon was hidden. Before coming to trial, Frye recanted this confession, but on July 20, 1922, he was convicted of second-degree murder and sentenced to life imprisonment. Frye appealed his convictions on grounds that, on June 10, 1922, he had submitted to a test conducted by Dr. William M. Marston designed to establish if he [Frye] was telling the truth. The test was carried out using a sphygmomanometer, a device used to measure blood pressure, and it amounted to an early and very rudimentary form of polygraph or "lie detector." According to the Frye defense team, the results indicated that Frye was telling the truth when he said that he had not killed Brown. But the court had refused to admit this evidence, and on December 3, 1923, the Court of Appeals of District of Columbia agreed. They wrote, "Just when a scientific principle or discovery crosses the line between the experimental and demonstrable stages is difficult to define . . . the thing from which the deduction is made must be sufficiently established to have gained general acceptance in the particular field in which it belongs."[2] Later, in the same opinion, they wrote: "We think the systolic blood pressure deception test has not yet gained such standing and scientific recognition among physiological and psychological authorities as would justify the courts in admitting expert testimony deduced from the discovery, development, and experiments thus far made."[3] The judgment was affirmed and Frye served the remainder of his life sentence, little realizing that he had gained a place in legal history.

(a fast-tracking of the judicial process that forgoes the need for a trial), arguing that Bendectin had not caused the child's disorder. The court sided with Merrell Dow, finding that Daubert's experts had relied on evidence "not sufficiently established to have general acceptance in the field to which it belongs."[4]

In essence *Daubert v. Merrell Dow Pharmaceuticals, 509 U.S. 579 (1993)* sounded eerily similar to *Frye*, but the court went further. It decided that the *Frye* test was superseded by the 1975 Federal Rules of Evidence. These were 11 articles, with several subsections, that were designed to govern the admission of facts in federal courts. (Although formally adopted by the Congress, the Federal Rules of Evidence were not binding on individual states. However, the rules of many states have been closely modeled on these provisions.) In *Daubert*, the Supreme Court singled out Rule 702, which dealt with expert testimony, and which, in its original form, stated: "If scientific, technical, or other specialized knowledge will assist the trier of fact to understand the evidence or determine a fact in issue, a witness qualified as an expert by knowledge, skill, experience, training, or education, may testify thereto in the form of an opinion or otherwise."

In adopting Rule 702 as its guideline, the Supreme Court decided that the presiding judge should be the "gatekeeper" of what was "relevant" and "reliable" when it came to scientific testimony. Many felt this was a step too far, placing an unfair burden on the judges, obliging them to pass judgment on areas of science in which they have no expertise. Others shrugged, feeling that not much had changed. Indeed, one commentator has scathingly dismissed *Daubert* as "Frye in drag."[5] It is widely believed that the Supreme Court, in adopting *Daubert*, was making an attempt to try to banish what it considered to be "junk science" from the courtroom. Ever since the 1970s some legal academics had been arguing that too many lawsuits were being settled on the testimony of dubious expert witnesses. *Daubert* was supposed to remedy that situation. The jury is still out on whether that goal has been achieved.

So, having had its admissibility established legally, the evidence is then presented to the jury. They are the sole arbiters of its merit. It is their duty to listen to the evidence presented by both sides and to reach a verdict on that evidence alone. Nothing else is supposed to influence their judgment. But, of course, this makes little allowance for human nature. Juries are made up of disparate personalities and it is abundantly clear that two people can listen to exactly the same evidence and reach diametrically opposed conclusions. There is nothing the system can do to legislate this subjectivity out of existence. This is why evidence needs to be processed as accurately as possible, and presented to the court as accurately as possible. Anything else would lead to anarchy. In the cases covered in this book, many contentious issues arose over the manner in which evidence of various types was presented. All were resolved. This might not have been the case barely a century ago, for the methodical harvesting of evidence is a fairly new concept. To understand better where things are today, it is necessary to first understand when and why people in the past first began gathering evidence.

The History of Evidence

On the afternoon of March 15, 44 B.C., the most powerful man on earth entered the Senate in Rome. Julius Caesar ruled an empire that stretched from the eastern Mediterranean to the northernmost tip of England, but all that counted for naught on that momentous day. Without warning, a mob of knife-wielding senators suddenly rushed the hated dictator. It was all over in seconds. The mighty Caesar vanished beneath a hail of blows. According to the historian and biographer, Suetonius, Caesar's blood-drenched body was removed from the Senate floor and taken away for examination by a Greek physician named Antistius. He found that Caesar had sustained no fewer than 23 knife wounds. It had been a frenzied attack, no doubt about it, but Antistius reckoned that only one wound was fatal. With this finding, Antistius carved a notch in history—he had carried out the first recorded autopsy. He was also, unconsciously or not, searching for evidence.

Moving on a century, still in Rome, and we have Nero's mother, the ferociously ambitious Agrippina, accusing her rival, Lollia Paulina, of black magic. Poor Lollia didn't stand a chance. Denied any kind of hearing, she first had her property confiscated and was then banished from Rome. And things only got worse. The vengeful Agrippina reportedly ordered Lollia to commit suicide, and told her soldiers to bring back the severed head as proof that she was dead. By the time the head arrived in Rome, putrefaction was far advanced and Agrippina found

17

identification impossible, until she examined the teeth and, on finding a distinctively discolored front tooth, realized that her hated enemy would trouble her no more. Again, Agrippina was looking for evidence, this time to provide proof of identity. Only then was she convinced.

TRIAL BY ORDEAL

After this promising start, the search for evidence tailed off disappointingly. Instead, for most of the next two millennia, just the merest hint of suspicion was enough to land one in hot water—often literally. Trial by ordeal was a ghastly procedure in which God was appealed to as the highest judge. Exactly what form this ordeal took was decided by the earthbound judges, and a ghoulishly imaginative bunch they turned out to be. Invariably the accused was subjected to burning with hot oil or fire, being pressed with scalding irons, or else having to endure unfeasibly long periods of immersion in water. If, after a few days, a priest decided that any wounds had healed satisfactorily, then that defendant was adjudged innocent. Similarly if he survived the attempt to drown him. The assumption was made that God, with His mastery of the two great elements of fire and water, would dictate guilt or innocence. Trial by battle, although less common, followed much the same principle. God was always assumed to be on the side of right, even if that principle tended to be embodied in the stronger combatant.

As trial by ordeal fell into disfavor, and courts shifted from the religious to the secular, evidence began to assume a more important role in the judicial process. Mostly, it took the form of either eyewitness testimony or confession. How some of these confessions were obtained left much to be desired. For instance, when Guy Fawkes—who in November 1605 attempted to blow up the British Houses of Parliament—was arrested and hauled off to the Tower of London, he was shackled to an instrument called the rack, a particularly nasty collection of ropes, rollers, and pulleys that could yank limbs from their sockets. Fawkes bravely held out for four days before finally giving up the names of some co-conspirators. He was later executed, but his trial had been a farce. Like most defendants at the time, his guilt was already taken for granted. Any prisoner hoping to escape the wrath of the law was expected to prove his or her innocence. This unsatisfactory state of affairs persisted for centuries and didn't really come under serious attack until the early 19th century.

This was when science entered the scene. It was, admittedly, a rudimentary form of science, but it was a start. Early breakthroughs in toxicological analysis resulted in a string of sensational Victorian poisoning cases being brought to trial, none of which would have seen the light of day a century earlier. Not all of the outcomes were satisfactory. But the search was now on for more accurate methods of finding and analyzing evidence. Probably the greatest breakthrough came with the discovery that no two humans share the same fingerprints. For the first time, law enforcement agencies had a definitive means of telling one person from another. Prior to this, investigators had relied on **bertillonage**, a system of identification based on dozens of different human measurements. Now this was consigned to the scrap heap.

As the 20th century dawned, it was the turn of the serologists to take center-stage. First came the Austrian scientist, Karl Landsteiner, who in 1901 discovered the ABO blood grouping system that would later win him the 1930 Nobel Prize. Hot on his heels came Paul Uhlenhuth, a German biologist, who devised a means of distinguishing human blood from that of other animals. These were huge advances in the field of evidence processing, and the results were soon seen in the courts. Killers who would once have walked free, now found themselves walking to the gallows.

But it wasn't all one-way traffic. The courts were proving to be highly resistant to the introduction of some forms of scientific evidence. Chief among these was the polygraph, or so-called lie detector. Throughout history, mankind has searched for ways to trap liars. Priests in India (c. 500 B.C.) would herd suspected thieves into a darkened room with a "magic donkey," whose tail had been daubed with lampblack. The suspects were then ordered to pull the donkey's tail, having been warned that when the genuine thief pulled the tail, the magic donkey would speak and be heard throughout the temple. When the room was emptied a few minutes later, the person who still had clean hands—having not pulled the tail—was declared the thief and punished.

China came up with an even simpler method. Suspected liars were fed a handful of dry rice. If they could spit it out, so the reasoning went, they were telling the truth; if the rice stuck to their tongue, they were thought to have something to hide.

As crude as it may seem, this Chinese "truth test" employed exactly the same principle as the modern polygraph—the notion that when people lie, their body reacts in ways that they are unable to control. Whereas Chinese interrogators were on the lookout for a dry mouth as an indicator of lying, the polygraph operator searches for deception by studying changes in blood pressure, rates of breathing, pulse, and perspiration.

HOW THE POLYGRAPH WORKS

The polygraph works by attaching rubber tubes to the subject's chest, a blood pressure cuff to the arm, and small metal plates to the fingers. The examiner then asks the subject a series of questions. The polygraph measures various physical responses, including respiration, perspiration, and blood pressure. These responses are plotted on a graph.

How the questions are framed is critical. Because individuals react differently, the examiner needs to know what triggers a "lie" response in that particular subject. To this end, each test contains certain "control" questions, to which the subject is directed to answer untruthfully. The induced anxiety usually shows as a blip on the graph. Once this untruthful benchmark has been established, the actual test can begin.

Numerous questions are fired at the subject. Each response is assigned a number from -3 (indicating a strong negative correlation) to +3 (indicating a strong positive correlation), measured by comparing the relevant response to the previously established "controls." Once all the responses are added together, a total score of +6 or greater suggests that the subject is lying.

While no one disputes that polygraphs measure perceptible changes in human response, there can be no absolute guarantee that these changes are prompted by the act of lying.

LIE DETECTORS

The first recorded attempt to construct a mechanical device to measure emotion and determine truth and deception can be traced to the noted criminologist, Cesare Lombroso. As early as 1885 he was assisting the Italian police, interviewing suspects, and recording changes in blood pressure as a means of establishing the truth. The next innovation in lie detection came in 1913 when another Italian, psychologist Vittorio Benussi, published a paper on using breath measurement as a means of determining truthfulness.

Because stress plays a big factor in any polygraph test—even truthful subjects occasionally send the styluses haywire—much depends on how the examiner interprets the data. And herein lies much of the controversy. Give the same polygraph results to two different examiners and, as tests have shown, it is entirely possible that they will reach opposing conclusions as to the subject's truthfulness.

Supporters of the polygraph argue that a properly trained examiner will catch 95 percent of all liars. Critics put the figure much lower, and say that, with minimal practice, almost anyone can be taught how to "beat the machine" by deliberately manipulating their physiological responses to give false positives. To back up their skepticism they cite the case of Aldrich Ames, the notorious CIA agent who, in 1994, was convicted of spying for the Soviet Union and later Russia, after having twice "passed" polygraph screenings.

Despite these misgivings, the polygraph remains a potent weapon in the American crime fighting arsenal. Even the courts are beginning to relax their prohibition, with some states now permitting the limited introduction of polygraph results as evidence. However, in 1998, the United States Supreme Court restated its distrust of the polygraph in *United States v. Scheffer, 118 S. Ct. 1261*, when it affirmed the judgment of an army court-martial in refusing to admit the results of a polygraph examination into evidence.

In the First World War an American scientist engaged in counter-intelligence, William Marston, took the process one step further, developing a systolic blood pressure gauge that he tested on German POWs. Unimpressed with his results, Marston discontinued its use.

Despite all these forerunners, most consider the "Father of the Polygraph" to be John Larson, a medical student at the University of California at Berkeley. In 1920, working in close conjunction with his local police chief, August Vollmer, Larson built the first machine specifically designed to detect lying through plotting simultaneous measurements of blood pressure, pulse, and respiration on graph paper. Larson decided to call his machine a polygraph, in recognition of a Scottish cardiologist, Sir James Mackenzie, who several years previously, had designed a multifunction heart monitor that he called a *polygraph* (from the Greek for *many writings*).

Although immediately popular with police departments across America, the polygraph suffered a major judicial setback when, as described in the Introduction, the United States Supreme Court ruled unproven scientific testimony to be legally inadmissible. As a result the polygraph was largely barred from the courtroom, even as its use in everyday life mushroomed, especially in the sphere of job applications. But science, having gained a foothold in the courtroom, was in no mood to simply vanish. And nobody grasped this reality more than the criminals themselves. Professional housebreakers began wearing gloves to conceal their fingerprints and they took care to avoid leaving any blood at crime scenes. But their immunity was short-lived. Science delivered the **spectrograph,** which enabled investigators to identify fibers shed from those gloves. Then the chromatograph was used to analyze blood samples at ever greater levels of accuracy. Before long, analysts were even able to match bullets to the guns that had fired them. At every turn, the avenues of escape for the criminal were being closed. But scientific evidence is only as good as the person who gathers or analyzes it. And that person needs to be able to convince a jury. Cue the introduction of the expert witness.

EXPERT WITNESSES

They first came to courtroom prominence at the beginning of the 20th century. Before this, most scientific-based testimony was medical in

A lie detector operator tests a female subject. Law-enforcement officials use the polygraph machine during investigations, but the results cannot be used as evidence in a court of law. *Bob Daemmrich/The Image Works*

nature, and delivered almost exclusively by doctors or professors. But the flurry of new crime fighting developments saw the introduction of experts from outside the medical arena. Most were ethical and motivated by a desire to advance the cause of their specialty. Others saw only dollar bills. For them, the role of expert witness was a passport to easy street. One of the earliest—and certainly the most notorious—was a Buffalo-based druggist named Albert H. Hamilton. What Hamilton didn't know about science wasn't worth knowing; or so he claimed. In his slickly produced publicity brochure, "That Man

A BODY OF EVIDENCE

Autopsies have come a long way since the time of Antistius. Although all medical examiners employ slightly different techniques, the following 10-step process is typical of most criminal autopsies:

1. The body arrives at the mortuary in a bag, with the extremities wrapped in plastic to ensure that evidence is not lost in transit. A general description of the body is made, covering height, weight, general condition, and any obvious external wounds. Any clothing is then removed and bagged for further analysis.
2. A full external examination of the front of the body now takes place. Typically this might start at the head and neck, then proceed to the chest, the abdomen, upper limbs, lower limbs, and genitalia. The whole procedure is repeated for the back.
3. Next, trace evidence is gathered from the body. This includes fingernail scrapings or clippings. In sex crime cases, swabs are taken at key locations. Swabs also figure prominently in gunshot cases, as samples from around the wound might reveal powder residue that may provide a clue as to the range at which the shot was fired.
4. Photographs are taken. A ruler is included in every photograph so that the size of any wound is obvious, to prevent any subsequent disputes.

from Auburn," which landed on the desk of just about every practicing attorney in upstate New York in the early 20th century, Hamilton outlined his fields of expertise. These included: chemistry, **microscopy**, handwriting, ink analysis, typewriting, photography, fingerprints, **toxicology**, gunshot wounds, revolvers, guns and cartridges, bullet identification, gunpowder, **nitroglycerine**, dynamite, high explosives, blood and other stains, cause of death, embalming fluids, determination of the distance a revolver was held when discharged, **ballistics** analysis, and several others. The list ran on and on, finally

5. The body is opened using a Y-shaped incision from shoulders to mid-chest and down to the groin.

6. This incision enables easy access to the thorax and neck, and exposes any **subcutaneous** bruising that might not be apparent on the surface of the skin. Close attention is paid to the neck, always one of the body's most vulnerable and informative regions.

7. The breastbone is cut through, exposing the organs of the chest, from which tissue is saved and sent for analysis. All the organs are weighed carefully.

8. A single incision is made across the top of the head, and the scalp is pulled forward and backward to reveal the skull. A special vibrating saw, that cuts bone but not soft tissue, is used to cut through the skull, and the dome is pried off.

9. Once the skull is open, the brain can be removed. In cases involving blunt instruments, skull fragments should match damage to the meninges—the membrane around the brain—and to the surface of the brain itself.

10. After completion of the autopsy, the body is reconstructed by reversing the dissection process. The breastbone and ribs are usually replaced in the body; the skull and trunk incisions are sewed shut, using the trademark "baseball stitch," the body is washed, and then responsibility passes to the undertakers.

running out of breath only when it had reached the staggering total of 26 specialties!

Hamilton might have been brash, but he was smart and he was a brilliant salesman. Somehow he managed to parlay a smattering of scientific knowledge into a highly profitable business. At a time when an average American worker considered himself fortunate if he earned $50 a month, Hamilton regularly raked in that much per day, plus expenses. For this, he would say pretty much whatever his paymasters—mainly prosecutors—wanted him to say. He was always careful to litter his testimony with obscure scientific terms. The advantages were twofold; not only did it help mask his ignorance, it also impressed the heck out of juries. Hamilton might have been a small man, but he always punched way above his weight on the witness stand. His resilience under cross-examination was awesome, another reason for his continued success. Some courts did see through him, however. In 1911, during one hotly contested libel suit arising from newspaper accusations that he had tampered with evidence, Hamilton's witness-stand pomposity so incensed spectators that they chased the startled little druggist from the court. Mostly, though, he managed to fool the courts, often with terrifying results. In 1916, an innocent farmhand named Charles Stielow came within 45 minutes of the electric chair, on the back of some phony ballistics testimony that Hamilton had cooked up. Stielow was reprieved and later pardoned. And during a 1924 review of the notorious Sacco and Vanzetti convictions, Hamilton, who'd been hired by the defense, was actually caught trying to switch the barrel on the murder weapon. Despite these blips, Hamilton continued to testify and to draw big paychecks from prosecutors and defenders alike until his death in 1938.

His legacy lives on. Crooked, or simply inept, expert witnesses are the bane of the legal system. In the 1980s, Fred Zain rose to the position of Chief of **Serology** at the West Virginia Department of Public Safety (the state crime lab). As an expert witness, he testified in hundreds of criminal cases, especially those tough ones that the prosecutors were unsure about. Like Hamilton, Zain was a formidable courtroom performer. He knew how to carry the jury with him. His reputation reached across state borderlines and the job offers rolled in. Eventually he took a more prestigious post in Bexar County, Texas. The move had no discernible impact on his success rate. Zain seemed able to find the evidence that no one else could uncover. There was just one problem: Fred Zain was a fraud. His academic background was modest; for instance, he had failed organic chemistry, one of his claimed areas of expertise and that he routinely testified about. Incredibly, nobody had bothered to check his qualifications. It turned out that plenty of people had expressed doubts about Zain over the years, but their criticisms had either been ignored or, in some cases, the complainants had even been fired. When the bubble did finally burst, a special investigation ordered by the West Virginia Supreme Court concluded that Zain's false testimony was directly responsible for six wrongful convictions. These men were subsequently freed. When news of Zain's tainted past emerged, Bexar County authorities promptly fired him. The discredited chemist was under indictment in December 2002, when he died from cancer.

The list goes on. Joseph Kopera, a Maryland firearms examiner, was another expert witness who was found to have repeatedly perjured himself when asked in court about his qualifications. In a career that spanned almost four decades, he worked at the Maryland state crime lab for 21 years before his duplicity was uncovered. On March 1, 2007, after having been confronted with evidence that he had forged his credentials, Kopera decided to take immediate retirement. That same day he shot himself.

Whether through reasons of ego, money, or pressure from above, too many expert witnesses have shown themselves to be dangerously fallible. Happily, these are in a minority. Overwhelmingly, the people who testify in court do so from the best of motives. They know the profound impact that their testimony can have. They also know that if justice is to be served, it is imperative that the evidence is harvested and analyzed with scrupulous attention to detail. Nothing else is acceptable.

2

Trace Evidence

Trace evidence is the generic term given to any type of physical clue found at a crime scene. It might be as large as a pool of blood or as tiny as a skin cell. Whatever its size, the sample must be processed with care and accuracy if its full evidential value is ever to be realized. Generally, trace evidence is gathered, bagged, and labeled by criminalists, skilled technicians with a keen awareness of the Locard Exchange Principle. Developed by the French scientist Edmond Locard, the Exchange Principle holds that whenever two human beings come into physical contact—no matter how briefly—something from one is transferred to the other. This has been crystallized in a single sentence: *Every contact leaves a trace.* Say, for instance, someone enters a room. Unconsciously that person might brush against a sofa and pick up a fiber on his or her clothing. Alternatively a transfer might occur in reverse; with the person shedding a fiber from his or her clothes and leaving it on the sofa. In this example two outcomes are inevitable; the room is forever altered and so is the item of clothing.

It all sounds deceptively simple, but for almost a century Locard's Exchange Principle has been the driving force of accurate crime scene processing. Find the evidence, investigators reason, and there is a good chance that it might lead to the criminal. First, though, they need to factor in the scarcity of the evidence. This applies right across the spectrum. If an iPod, say, is found at a crime scene, its evidential value is limited. There are millions in existence and even if the serial number can identify the original purchaser, this is by no means proof that the purchaser was present at the crime scene. The iPod might have since been sold, stolen, or simply lost. However, if the item found happens to be a shirt button, and if the suspect owns a shirt that is missing just such a button, then this is far more incriminating. It's all a question of rarity. The scarcer the evidence, the greater its courtroom value. Few investigations demonstrate this principle quite so vividly as the hunt for the notorious Atlanta Child Killer.

REIGN OF TERROR BEGINS

In July 1979 someone began murdering young black males in the city of Atlanta, Georgia. Over the next 22 months the bodies of 28 victims, ranging in age from seven to 28, were found in and around the city. Most had been strangled or asphyxiated. Some showed signs of having been stabbed or battered to death. The crime scenes were frustratingly free from clues, until investigators began gathering small fibers and dog hairs from the bodies and clothing of many of the victims. These were forwarded to the Georgia State Crime Laboratory. Two types of fiber were isolated: yellow-green nylon and violet acetate rayon. Interest, initially, focused on the yellow-green fibers. They were highly unusual, coarse with a trilobed—triangular in shape with convex sides—cross-sectional appearance, of a kind associated with carpets or rugs. Photographic enlargements of the fibers were circulated among various textile manufacturers, but no one in the industry could identify them. It was a similar story when investigators showed the same photographs to a convention of chemists. All agreed that the fibers were exceptionally unusual and all were united in their ignorance of the fibers' source.

Such a concentration on fiber analysis inevitably found its way into the media. On February 11, 1981, an Atlanta newspaper carried details of the research. This sparked a significant development. The murderer, in a break from his previous routine, suddenly began dumping his victims in rivers. Also, they were now either nude or barely clothed. This strongly suggested that the serial killer was monitoring media coverage of his activities and modifying his *modus operandi* accordingly. He thought he was being smart, but then he blundered.

At approximately 2:50 A.M. on May 22, 1981, a four-man surveillance team staking out the Chattahoochee River in northwest Atlanta—one of the killer's favored dumping grounds for his victims—heard a loud splash. They spotted a station wagon cruising slowly away from the James Jackson Parkway Bridge. After being tailed for a mile, the driver, Wayne Williams, a 23-year-old black music promoter, was pulled over and questioned. He admitted stopping by the bridge, but he claimed he had merely used a phone booth to call a young woman whom he was hoping to audition. (It was later learned that the phone number Williams gave officers had been out of commission since August 1978.) After an hour's questioning, Williams was allowed to leave.

Two days later the strangled body of Nathaniel Cater, 27, was dragged from the river a mile downstream from the bridge; in his hair was a single yellow-green carpet fiber. Suddenly, all investigative eyes turned toward the slick-talking impresario. On June 3, acting on a search warrant, investigators raided Williams's home on Penelope Road in northwest Atlanta, where he lived with his parents. What struck them immediately was that, throughout the house, the floor was covered with a distinctive, yellow-green carpeting. Also, the family kept a dog, potentially the source of the hairs that had been found on some bodies.

With no direct evidence to connect Williams to the Atlanta slayings—there were claims that he was homosexual and had been seen with one of the victims shortly before his death, but this was always hotly disputed—investigators realized that everything hinged on those yellow-green fibers. Generally, fiber evidence is corroborative to other evidence; here, it would be absolutely central to the case against Wayne Williams. Working with chemists at DuPont, America's largest producer of fibers, Federal Bureau of Investigation (FBI) analysts passed the yellow-green fibers recovered from the victims through a spinneret, a device that stretches the sample, giving it distinguishable optical characteristics. Although DuPont themselves made a trilobed carpet fiber, microscopic analysis show it to be markedly dissimilar to the crime scene sample. Originally it was thought that DuPont was the only company that made this kind of fiber, then it was learned that a Boston textile manufacturer, Wellman Inc., also produced a trilobed fiber. The company had developed its fiber as a less expensive alternative to the

A shaft of hair magnified by an electron microscope. Hairs found at a crime scene are analyzed in a laboratory to determine whether they are human or animal, and whether they came from the victim, the suspect, or are unrelated to the case. Hairs, microscopically similar to those from Wayne Williams's dog, were found on several of his victims. *Patrick Landmann/Photo Researchers, Inc.*

DuPont product. More significant still, under a microscope the Wellman fiber looked identical to the crime scene samples.

At this point it should be emphasized that science cannot specifically identify a manufactured fiber as coming from a particular source (similarly with dog hairs). All an analyst can say is that two samples are microscopically indistinguishable, which is what happened in this instance. Company records showed that this particular fiber—called Wellman 181B—had been made and sold to various carpet makers during the years 1967 through 1974. Because each carpet manufacturer has its own dyes and weaving techniques, it was possible to track these

INVENTOR OF THE GOLDEN RULE

Edmond Locard, the man who changed forever the face of forensic detection, was born in France in 1877. After receiving his early education at the Dominican College at Quillins, he attended the nearby University of Lyon. Here he fell under the spell of the faculty's Professor of Forensic Medicine, Alexandre Lacassagne, another great pioneer of scientific detection. Lacassagne soon recognized Locard's abilities and took the young man under his wing. Locard was a brilliant student. After graduating as Doctor of Medicine and also Licentiate in Law, he became Lacassagne's assistant, holding the post until 1910, when he resigned to establish what would become the Laboratoire Intérregional de Police Technique in Lyon.

The rather grand-sounding title helped mask the fact that Locard's workplace was a modest two-room operation on the second floor of the Lyon courthouse, and that it housed only two items of equipment; a microscope and a spectroscope. Humble, maybe, yet here was the world's first dedicated medico-legal facility. All of the high-tech laboratories around the globe can trace their lineage back to these lowly beginnings.

What Locard lacked in equipment he more than made up for in drive and invention. Nothing was off-limits as he applied his considerable intellect to the business of crime solving. He studied handwriting; the formulation of a 12-point method of fibers to the West Point Pepperell Corporation of Dalton, Georgia. They had manufactured a line of carpeting known as Luxaire, and one of the colors offered was English Olive, which both visually and chemically matched the carpeting found at Williams's home.

While this finding undoubtedly cast great suspicion upon Williams, it was far from conclusive proof of guilt. After all, what was the statistical likelihood of the fibers having come from his carpet and his alone? Only the scarcity or otherwise of Luxaire English Olive could answer that question. For instance, if every house in the Atlanta metropolitan area were fitted with Luxaire English Olive, then its evidential value

fingerprint identification; as well as making innovative analyses of body fluids, hair, and skin. Most unusually for the time, he wasn't hidebound by academic snobbery; always he urged his students to read the Sherlock Holmes novels, which he regarded as classic exemplars of logic and reasoning.

But it is in the field of trace evidence where Locard gained immortality. His exchange principle—that *"every contact leaves a trace"*—has become the golden rule of forensic detection. Enter a room or brush against another person, said Locard, and you either leave something there that was previously on your person, or you take something away with you. Millions of convicted criminals on every continent can attest to the accuracy of Locard's truism.

As Locard's fame grew, so did his responsibilities. He became the founding director of the Institute of Criminalistics at the University of Lyon. He also taught and wrote voluminously on his subject, and in 1912 he published the first volume of his monumental treatise *Traité de Criminalistique*. Within its pages he argued that proof is established in a criminal trial by confession, presumption, written evidence, testimony, and scientific evidence. The core of his work he summed up in a single oft-repeated phrase: "To write the history of identification is to write the history of criminology." Following his retirement in 1951, Locard continued his research, and remained active until his death in 1966.

would be nil. On the other hand, should that particular carpet be found in Williams's house and nowhere else, then any reasonable jury would have to regard that as highly significant. Somewhere between these polar extremes lay the statistical probability. Investigators needed to nail down some numbers.

Although Luxaire was manufactured from 1970 through 1975, it used Wellman 181B fiber for just one 12-month period between 1970 and 1971. During that time, 16,397 square yards of Luxaire English Olive were sold by West Point Pepperell to retail outlets across 10 southeastern states, including Georgia. Compared with the 1979 total U.S. residential carpeted floor space, estimated by DuPont at *6.7 billion square yards*, this was a minuscule amount of carpet.

WHAT ARE THE ODDS?

These were the indisputable facts. In order to establish the statistical probability of Luxaire English Olive being found in any one residence, certain conservative assumptions had to be made: first, that sales of Luxaire English Olive were evenly distributed throughout all 10 states, and that it was only installed in one room, average size 12 feet by 15 feet. Erring heavily on the side of caution and fairness, investigators next assumed that all the 10-year-old carpet was still in use (although this was most unlikely, since the average life span of most commercial dwelling carpet is four to five years). This allowed them to calculate that, in Georgia, one could expect to find 82 homes containing the carpet. Since at the time of Williams's arrest there were 638,995 occupied housing units in metropolitan Atlanta alone, the odds of randomly selecting a home in that city with one room carpeted in Luxaire English Olive were 1 in 7,792—a very low probability indeed. Put another way, in order to randomly pick up the fiber found in his hair, Nathaniel Cater would have had to visit almost 8,000 houses in Atlanta or just one—the home of Wayne Williams.

There was one troubling factor. Lab technicians had noticed some slight color variation between the carpet in Williams's house and those fibers recovered from the river, which appeared to have been bleached. By subjecting various known samples of the carpet to small amounts of Chattahoochee River water for different periods of time, a similar bleaching effect was achieved.

Although Williams was the prime suspect in as many as 28 murders, prosecutors felt their best chances of conviction rested with just two cases: Nathaniel Cater and Jimmy Ray Payne, 21, whose half-naked body had been recovered from the Chattahoochee River on April 27, 1981. Again they were pinning their hopes on fiber analysis: bedspread, carpet, blanket, and bathroom rug fibers found on Payne's head all matched fibers in the Williams house and there was something else—a single fragment of violet-colored rayon found on Payne's red shorts. This was microscopically indistinguishable to the carpeting in Wayne Williams's 1970 Chevrolet station wagon. Investigators asked Chevrolet for details of all the pre-1973 cars that had been fitted with this kind of carpet. When the answer came back the Georgia licensing authorities clarified how many of these vehicles were registered in the Atlanta metropolitan area in 1981. Out of 2,373,512 registered cars, just 620 met the criteria. This result of 1 in 3,828 also provided the statistical likelihood of Payne having acquired the fiber by random contact with any other car except that belonging to Williams.

At this point the numbers began soaring exponentially. Investigators took the odds against Cater having picked up the fiber randomly—1 in 7,792—and multiplied them with the possibility that the rayon fragment found on Payne's shorts had an equally random origin, 1 in 3,828. The laws of probability say that this will occur no more than once in every 29,827,776 times! And yet both types of fiber were found in debris vacuumed from Williams's station wagon.

Further strengthening the connection to Williams is the fact that transferred fibers are usually lost rapidly as people go about their daily routine. This meant that Cater and Payne almost certainly picked up the fibers either shortly before or at the time of their deaths. Also, the locations of the various fibers—on Payne's shorts and Cater's head and pubic hair—were not places where fibers would have been transferred from a house or car to the victims had they been fully clothed. These findings supported prosecution claims that Williams was an aggressive homosexual who had deliberately targeted vulnerable young men.

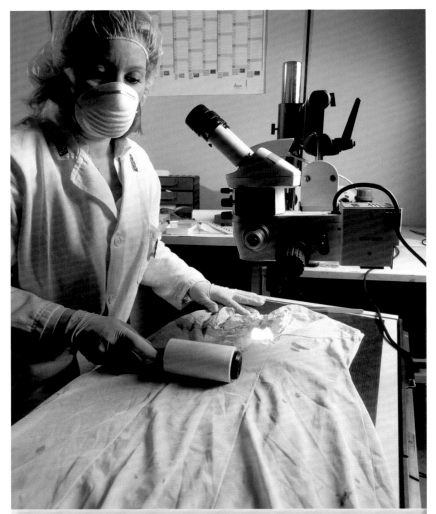

A forensic investigator uses an adhesive roller to collect hair and fibers from a dress. Further analysis may link the evidence to a suspect. Such analysis was crucial in the conviction of Wayne Williams. *Mauro Fermariello/Photo Researchers, Inc.*

When the case came to trial in January 1982, the prosecution was allowed to introduce evidence regarding other alleged victims of the Atlanta Child Killer. This took the form of a chart that listed, in chronological order, the deaths of 12 young persons. On each body were found between three and six fibers and dog hairs that could be traced to either

Williams's home or automobile. The odds against such a likelihood—virtually incalculable—ran into the trillions. To help the jury make sense of these mind-boggling numbers the prosecution prepared more than 40 charts and 350 photographs. There was also evidence that two of these other victims, John Porter and William Barrett, showed signs

WILLIAMS: KILLER OR VICTIM?

Oddly enough, the man dubbed the Atlanta Child Killer was actually convicted of killing two adult males. This anomaly only fueled suspicions in certain quarters that Williams had been victimized by a racist police force, intent on pinning all 28 murders on an innocent black man, instead of investigating allegations that Ku Klux Klan members had waged a campaign to exterminate young black males. An absence of publicly available evidence to support these claims was also blamed on the authorities, with Williams's supporters contending that the state had deliberately suppressed evidence that could have led to an acquittal. This argument finally received a judicial airing in 2005. After listening carefully to arguments from both sides, U.S. District Judge Beverly Martin delivered her decision on February 8, 2006. She wrote that none of the allegedly withheld evidence "would have had more than a minimal impact upon the outcome of Mr. Williams's trial had it been presented to the jury."[1]

Looking beyond any perceived racial bias—an oft-over-looked fact is that the jury was made up of eight blacks and four whites—most of the complaints have centered on the fact that Williams was convicted "only" on circumstantial evidence. As the statistics quoted in the prosecution's case illustrate, an overwhelming barrage of circumstantial evidence is often the very best evidence of all. Those who protested that Williams was tried more by the law of probabilities than the law of the land would do well to bear in mind that, for the most part, juries are comprised of sensible citizens, and that there are only so many coincidences they are prepared to swallow.

of having been stabbed, and that blood found in the Chevrolet station wagon matched their blood types. But it was the fiber evidence that doomed Wayne Williams.

Defense claims that these fibers could have been transferred to Cater and Payne after their bodies were thrown into the river crumbled in the face of testimony that identical fibers were found on victims whose bodies had been recovered from several different locations.

After an eight-week trial, it was time for the case to go to the jury. The anticipated lengthy deliberation actually took less than 12 hours. On February 27, 1982, Williams was convicted and sentenced to two life terms.

Direct Evidence

Direct evidence can take many forms. It might be a fingerprint, or a scrap of DNA, or maybe a burglar is caught in possession of items that are known to have been stolen. All of these are examples of evidence that can be directly linked to a single source. More controversially, direct evidence can also include eyewitness testimony. This kind of evidence can be notoriously unreliable.

Happily, not all forms of direct evidence are so compromised. Say a person is found shot dead in suspicious circumstances. If a bullet taken from the corpse can be matched to a particular firearm, then the possessor of that weapon is going to have some serious explaining to do. Similarly with fingerprints or DNA samples found at the crime scene. Each provides a definite link between A and B, where A is the crime and B is the suspect. All these are examples of rock solid direct evidence that will, most likely, lead to a conviction. But sometimes, as the following case demonstrates, direct evidence can turn up in the most unexpected places.

On a scorching hot south Texas day in July 1982, the police in Santa Rosa, a sleepy town about 35 miles northwest of Brownsville, received a strange call. A member of the public had spotted an abandoned car, perched precariously on the edge of a drainage canal just outside town. When officers arrived at the scene it was immediately apparent that the inside of the vehicle had been gutted by fire. Their suspicions were further heightened when the car was towed onto level ground; a large stone had been wedged on the gas pedal in a failed attempt to drive the car into the water. Also, someone had plastered mud all over the steering wheel, presumably in an effort to get rid of any fingerprints. Registration records showed the owner as a local construction foreman, Billy Staton, 26, who along with his 26-year-old fiancée, Leticia Castro, a fourth-grade teacher at Buckner Elementary School in Pharr, hadn't been seen for 10 days. A wide-ranging search of the canals and brushland that interlace this region of the Rio Grande Valley failed to provide any further clues.

Leticia's brother had last seen the couple on July 16, the day they left to pick up Staton's two-year-old daughter Melanie from his ex-wife. He explained that Staton was caught up in a long-running battle over child visitation rights, and that things had been getting ugly of late. When detectives called at the house of Staton's former wife, Sherry, and her new husband, Paul Wolf, both age 21, they learned that the couple had suddenly moved house on July 17, one day after the disappearance. The Wolfs were traced to nearby La Feria. Both insisted that Staton had never showed up to collect his daughter.

A search of the Wolfs' former residence revealed something strange, a damp spot in the middle of the living room carpet. Underneath the carpet a large section of the floor had been covered in yellow paint. Analysis of this stain confirmed the presence of blood, but the high level of paint contamination made the blood impossible to type. Even so, there was no disguising the fact that a large quantity of blood had been spilt at some time in this room, a feeling reinforced by the subsequent discovery of tiny, almost unnoticeable flecks of blood spatter on the walls. These told of some brutal struggle.

The evidence kept on coming. Out in the yard there was an area of freshly turned earth, such as might result from a stone or rock being pulled from the ground. When the large stone used to weight down the gas pedal was fitted into the empty space, it was like slotting the last piece in a jigsaw. When confronted by this development, Wolf abruptly changed his story.

He now admitted that Staton *had* shown up on the day in question, ready to take his daughter on a picnic, only to turn violent when told that Sherry and the child were not at home. Staton had come at him, swinging punches, said Wolf. By the greatest of good fortune Wolf happened to have an iron bar handy in the living room, which he used to defend himself. A flurry of blows left Staton motionless on the carpet. Moments later, Leticia burst in, saw what had happened, and she, too, had attacked Wolf. For the second time in a matter of minutes, Wolf was obliged to employ the iron bar in self-defense, with equally lethal results.

Panic-stricken, Wolf had then enlisted the assistance of a local mechanic and close friend, Glenn Henderson, 19, to help dispose of the bodies. They had used Staton's car. After first dumping the bodies in two separate drainage ditches, they drove several miles to another canal. Here, they rested the stone on the gas pedal of Staton's car, only for the engine to stall at the water's edge, leaving the car maddeningly high and dry. The next day, Wolf had gone back and torched the vehicle.

Wolf told detectives where the bodies could be found. On August 6, just one day before she and Staton had intended to marry, Leticia's body was recovered from a Rio Grande Valley drainage canal, some 12 miles away from the car, with her head stoved in. Ten miles in another direction, officers found Staton's body, partially submerged in a canal. His head was similarly crushed.

Thus far, Wolf's story had panned out, except for one glaring inconsistency—besides being bludgeoned with a bar, Leticia had also been shot in the head.

Wolf had no explanation when officers grilled him over this development, just a dull insistence that both killings had been in self-defense. What he didn't know was that the officers had found something else. And this was legal dynamite.

THE TELLTALE TAPE

Taped to Billy Staton's stomach was a mini-cassette recorder. He had worn it on the advice of his lawyer, to gain evidence of Sherry's foul-mouthed and malicious obstructionism whenever Staton came to collect his daughter on weekends. The intention was to demonstrate how Sherry was prepared to violate a court order that allowed him child visitation rights. Had the tape recorder now been a witness to murder?

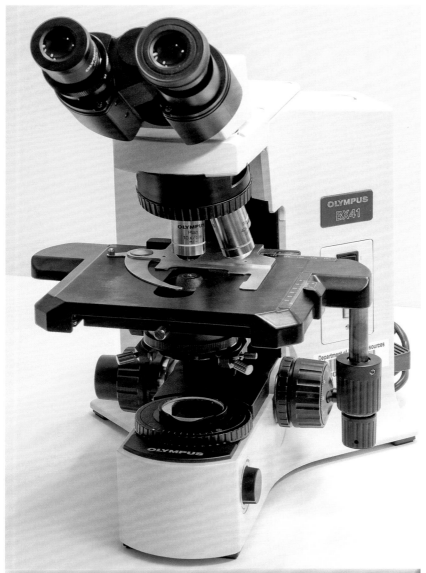

The compound light microscope is an essential tool for analyzing trace evidence. *Richard J. Green/Photo Researchers, Inc.*

By this time, the investigation was in the hands of the Texas Rangers. But they had no idea how to process a tape that had been submerged in water for several weeks. For this reason, Ranger Bruce Casteel contacted the FBI.

They instructed Casteel to send the tape—still immersed in water (this was essential; if exposed to air the tape might disintegrate)—to the FBI laboratory in Washington, D.C. When it arrived, FBI Agent Keith Sponholtz examined the tape carefully. There were obvious signs of degradation; much of the tape was moldy. As carefully as possible, Sponholtz made a copy of the original tape and worked with this alone. It was obvious, even on a first hearing, that it had, indeed, recorded Staton's visit to the Wolfs. But Sponholtz had to call on a variety of lab techniques and software packages in order to make the voices intelligible. He did this by juggling frequencies, lowering background noise, and enhancing the voices. Ten days later, the tape was back in Texas.

It provided a devastating record, what prosecutors would later call "23 minutes of murder,"[1] a fuzzy, but audible account of brutal homicide. It allowed investigators to go back to the house and by comparing elapsed times on the tape to the pattern of blood spatter on the walls—which by now had been matched to Staton's blood group—determine exactly what had happened.

Far from being bad-tempered, Staton had been quite calm as Wolf invited him in. It later emerged that Wolf had deliberately stacked piles of clothing on most of the living room furniture, leaving just one chair vacant. Paul was ushered to the chair, his back to the bedroom door. Sherry, too, was not away from the house, as Wolf had claimed, but clearly audible on the tape, talking to her ex-husband. Early on, Wolf made an excuse to take out some garbage; he needed to know if Leticia was waiting in the car outside. Once her presence was established, he returned to the house via the kitchen, where he picked up an iron bar, then crept into the living room behind Staton.

All this time, on the tape, Staton could be heard trying to persuade Melanie to go with him on a boating trip and picnic. She was crying, and several times said that she didn't want to go, only to then relent.

At this point, the conversation was interrupted by two distinct thuds, a groan, three more thuds, followed by the sound of Melanie crying and screaming. Then Wolf could be heard saying, "Get him. Get him, hurry up."[2]

Henderson confessed that the ambush had been planned in advance; that Wolf had approached him the previous day and told him of his homicidal intentions. And the tape supported this claim. Henderson now entered the entered the room. In the background a radio droned. After four minutes, another voice, that of Sherry, can be heard saying, "Get him up, get him out of here, the front door. Hit him again."[3] The tape then recorded five more thuds, interspersed with some moans. The next voice was that of Wolf: "Ah, Glenn, look at the mess you made."[4] A short while later he says, "Get the car . . . here right now."[5]

Together, Wolf and Henderson went out to deal with the unsuspecting Leticia. According to Henderson, Wolf climbed in the car and began strangling her, then hollered for Henderson to fetch a claw hammer and finish off the job by hitting Leticia on the head, which he did several times.

After Staton was hoisted into the trunk, the recorder captured the sounds of the car being driven off, as well as Staton's heavy breathing

MALICE THROUGH THE LOOKING GLASS

Most crime scenes yield some kind of trace evidence. It may be a scrap of fiber, a hair, some grit or powder, a flake of skin, or perhaps a pinpoint of mascara . . . the list is endless. What unites them all is their near invisibility. Without a microscope these fragments are evidentially worthless; put them under a magnifying lens, and they can become forensic gold dust.

No one knows for sure when the first compound microscope was made, but its invention is generally credited to a family of Dutch spectacle makers, Hans Jansen and his son Zacharias, sometime between 1590 and 1608. It was another Dutchman, Antonie van Leeuwenhoek, who revolutionized microscope technology. Disappointed by the crude compound microscopes then in existence, he built his own, using a single high quality lens. In 1673 he began writing letters to the Royal Society in London, describing research he had carried out on protozoa, bacteria, and red blood cells, all using his simple microscope. The dramatic nature of his discoveries stunned everyone. Leeuwenhoek's simple microscope held sway until and a loud gurgling noise that a pathologist testified was caused by blood in Staton's lungs. The final minutes of the tape record the breath and the life slowly seeping out of Staton's body.

Later on, when the two men were in the act of dumping the bodies, there came a startling realization—Leticia was still alive. Wolf ordered Henderson to shoot Leticia. He did so, with a single shotgun blast through the back of her head.

CHANGE OF PLEA

The effect of this tape upon Wolf was profound. His self-defense plea now flew out the window, replaced by a claim of temporary insanity. But he also had another obstacle to overcome; Henderson had worked out a deal with the state. In return for Henderson pleading

the 19th century when huge improvements in lens grinding allowed the compound microscope to regain its former status.

The very best types of modern optical microscopes permit magnifications as high as 2,000 times actual size (2,000x), powerful indeed, but not powerful enough for the requirements of contemporary forensic science. This craving for ever higher magnifications led researchers in the early 20th century to explore the possibility that cathode rays (or electrons) might be used in some way to increase microscope resolution.

This dream became reality in 1933 with the construction of the first true electron microscope. There are two basic types: the transmission electron microscope (TEM), which can only image specimens a fraction of a micrometer or less in thickness; and the scanning electron microscope (SEM), which is the type most used in forensic examination. In this process, a beam of electrons is scanned over the surface of a solid object. Enlargements of up to 150,000x are possible, though few forensic examinations require magnifications of such power.

No piece of forensic apparatus has led to the capture of more criminals than the microscope, and it remains the bedrock of evidence analysis.

guilty to the murder of Leticia Castro and agreeing to testify against Wolf, prosecutor Rey Cantu agreed to drop the Staton murder charge against him.

At Wolf's trial for murdering Leticia Castro—the Staton charge would be tried later—which began on April 11, 1983, his claim of temporary insanity received short shrift from several expert witnesses. Dr. Lee Coleman, a psychiatrist, testified that health professionals "do not have any special way of determining" whether someone was insane when he committed a violent act. "There is no science, no objectivity… that actually goes into the opinions that they're giving," he said. "There is nothing in our training that even vaguely gives us the ability to do something like that."[6]

VOICEPRINTS (VOICE RECOGNITION SPECTROGRAMS)

At the core of Sherry Wolf's defense was the claim that it wasn't her voice on the tape. Many experts question whether it is possible to identify a person through a recorded voice. As long ago as 1941, scientists at Bell Telephone Laboratories developed the sound spectrograph to test this theory. First used by World War II intelligence services to identify voices broadcast by German military communications, the technology fell into disuse until the early 1960s, when the FBI began to investigate its forensic applications. Bell engineer, Lawrence Kersta, became convinced that voice spectrograms, or "voiceprints" as he called them, could provide a valuable means of personal identification. Kersta's data was based on recordings of 50,000 different voices, many of them apparently similar. All showed great differences spectrographically.

The spectrograph records a 2.5-second band of speech and then scans it electronically—a process that takes 90 seconds. The output is next recorded onto a rotating drum. As the drum revolves, a filter adjusts the various frequencies, enabling a

Skepticism about Wolf's insanity claims extended to the bench. State District Judge Darrell Hester was notably unimpressed by the defendant's increasingly dull-witted courtroom performance, as Wolf began slurring his words and acting in a generally confused manner. He contrasted this with Wolf's sharp demeanor at the trial's outset, when he had responded lucidly to any questions. Attributing the decline either to drink, drugs, or downright bad acting, Hester revoked Wolf's $100,000 bail and ordered him jailed until the end of the trial. All this was done out of the jury's earshot. Hester had dismissed them just before blasting the defendant. "Mr. Wolf, if you think you've got 12 fools for a jury you're going to be sadly surprised," he thundered. "Any 10th-grader could see through the act. You're only hurting yourself."[7]

stylus to record their intensity. The resulting print contains a pattern of closely spaced lines showing all the audible frequencies in the recorded segment. The horizontal axis registers how high or low the voice is at that point; while volume is depicted by pattern density—the denser the print, the louder the tone. Two kinds of voiceprint can be obtained; bar prints and contour prints. The former are used for identification; while the contour version is suitable for computerized filing.

While the rate of voiceprint acceptance in American courtrooms has been sluggish, it has been used as **inceptive evidence** by the police, and has led to the capture of several criminals. Elsewhere, voice recognition spectrograms (VRS) are increasingly used in many areas of daily life. The U.S. military, always looking for more efficient ways of improving national security, now uses VRS as a means of monitoring access to restricted areas. Computer programmers, desperate to find the "killer app" that will enable the human voice to replace the keyboard and mouse, have also made quantum leaps in VRS software. Thus far, VRS has a claimed success rate of 99 percent, with professional impersonators able to defeat the system just 1 percent of the time. And it is that 1 percent that makes the use of this technology so controversial.

Grudgingly, Wolf yielded to the inevitable. While on the stand, he admitted that, two and a half months before the killings, he had paid $500 to have Staton beaten up, only for the hired thugs to run off with his money without fulfilling their side of the deal.

On April 20, 1983, after just 80 minutes of deliberation, the jury found Paul Wolf guilty of murder. He was sentenced to life imprisonment and fined $10,000. One month later, Wolf pleaded guilty to the murder of Staton and received a concurrent life term. The final member of this murderous trio, Sherry Wolf, failed in her attempts to convince the jury that she had been an innocent bystander. Once again the tape proved crucial. Her silence as she had left the room while her ex-husband was beaten to death was damning, as were her words on her return. Although Sponholtz said that it wasn't possible to scientifically identify the voice on the tape as that of Sherry—the defense argued that it was Wolf talking to Henderson—the jury had no doubt that she had been a willing party to murder. On July 29, 1983, she too was found guilty of murdering Staton and later imprisoned for life. Charges that she acted in the murder of Leticia Castro were dropped through a lack of evidence.

After the trial, Wolf's attorney, James Mardis, claimed that his client "would have had a very good chance of being acquitted had it not been for the tape."[8] While this might appear to be a somewhat overly optimistic appraisal of Wolf's prospects, there can be no doubt that the tape recording made conviction a formality. Some murderers have been known to tape their crimes, but what Staton did is probably unique. As direct evidence goes, it doesn't get much better. It was virtually tantamount to having Billy Staton stand up in court, pointing at the defendant and saying, "That man murdered me."

Trying to
Fool the Lab

According to the FBI,[1] in 2007 there were 14,831 homicides in the United States. Of these, just 10 victims died from the effects of deliberate poisoning. This astonishingly low number is open to various interpretations. It could mean that law enforcement agencies are not very good at investigating deaths by poison, with the result that many poisoners are escaping justice; or it might mean that modern toxicological analysis is now so sophisticated that few people think using poison is worth the effort. Certainly, any modern would-be poisoner would have to suffer from incurable optimism; because, if poisoning is suspected nowadays, it is virtually impossible for it to go undetected. But there's the rub; first of all, someone has to suspect that poison has been used. This is by no means as obvious as one might think. If someone, say, has a long history of ill-health, chances are that their death might not be scrutinized quite so closely as if they had been in tiptop physical shape. The same goes for someone of advanced age. Who knows how many elderly people have had their passage from this life eased by uncaring relatives?

It is a sobering thought that for most of recorded history, poisoners were able to dispense their potions, secure in the knowledge that they were impervious to detection. Only in the last 200 years has it become possible to trace poisons in the human body. Arsenic, with its ability to mimic the symptoms of so many potentially deadly gastric illnesses, was the poison of choice for centuries. It eventually succumbed to laboratory analysis, leading poisoners to seek out ever more obscure substitutes. Some are the stuff of legend, such as the minuscule **ricin** pellet injected by an assassin into the thigh of Bulgarian dissident Georgi Markov as Markov crossed a London bridge in 1978. Others, like **cyanide** and **prussic acid**, are more common, but no less lethal. All, though, are easily traceable in any modern forensic crime lab. Now, what the determined modern poisoner must do in order to avoid suspicion is to create a smokescreen. Devising a rather unique method of delivery helps also.

For years Janet Overton had been plagued by ill health. But just before noon on January 24, 1988, she felt well enough to join the rest of her family on a planned whale-watching expedition. No sooner did she step into the driveway of her home at Dana Point, California, than she collapsed. Even before the paramedics could arrive, the 46-year-old trustee of the Capistrano Unified School District was dead.

The autopsy found no reason to explain such a tragedy; but there again, Janet had been baffling the medical profession for years. Her health problems dated back to 1983, when she began losing prodigious amounts of weight. The tingling in her fingers, stomachaches, and a strange reddish-colored rash on her skin had all defied diagnosis. So, too, did the sores on her feet, so painful that she could barely walk at times. And now she was dead.

As a precautionary measure, blood and tissue samples were put into storage at the coroner's office before her body was released to the family. Husband Richard Overton, a 59-year-old computer consultant and occasional lecturer at the University of Southern California, opted for cremation.

For six months there were no further developments and then, in July, a middle-aged woman contacted the police. She had a disturbing tale to tell. Dorothy Boyer was Overton's first wife and she had read the accounts of Janet's death. Her initial response had been to push her suspicions very firmly to the back of her mind, but recently she and her daughter had visited Overton and made a surprising discovery. Hidden in a desk drawer were a syringe, rubber gloves, a container of some fluid, and a Revlon eyeliner.

The discoveries gave Dorothy a chill. These items resurrected memories of a grim episode from her past. Many years earlier, after divorcing Overton in 1967, her own health had gone into steep decline, so much so that she suspected her ex-husband, who still had access to the house, of poisoning her. Her suspicions had particularly been aroused by a strong sulfuric odor emanating from her shampoo. She also noticed that her symptoms occurred after drinking beverages that her children did not touch, such as coffee or wine. Again, each time when she smelt the cup or glass afterward she noticed that distinctive smell.

It was 1973 when Dorothy finally went to the police. She received a sympathetic hearing. Officers instructed her to mark the outside of a coffee container, which would reveal signs of tampering. Sure enough, three days later someone had removed the lid. Overton's fingerprints were found on the surface of the container, and analysis of its contents revealed the presence of **selenium**, a strong-smelling heavy metal, mixed with the coffee.

Overton's protestations of innocence, fiery at first, crumpled under questioning and he confessed. A deal was worked out: Dorothy agreed not to press charges if Overton stayed out of her life.

But all that had occurred 15 years previously. Was it possible that Richard Overton's warped habits had resurfaced and taken their toll on his second wife?

Initially, there appeared to be no reason why he would want Janet dead; the marriage seemed happy enough, he was financially independent, and the proceeds of Janet's life policy went to her son, not him. But slowly reports filtered through of Overton's almost insane jealousy. Friends said that Overton, holder of a doctorate in psychology, resented Jan's popularity and her clout with the Capistrano Unified School District, especially as she did not have a college degree. "He was just amazed that his wife could be elected," said one, "that she could be popular, and that she had this commanding, progressive presence in the district."[2]

There had also been frequent disputes over money. Janet had inherited $100,000 from her deceased mother and her determination to keep this money out of Overton's clutches had sparked a great deal of friction. But mostly, though, the marriage was foundering because of infidelity. Overton found out that Janet had been seeing two other men.

His anger found bizarre outlets. One man, who later admitted to having had a six-year-long affair with Janet, said that in 1984 Overton had had flyers produced proclaiming the affair, and that he had posted these flyers on car windshields during school functions.

A SECRET WIFE

Overton's jealousy was hard to stomach, given his own double-dealing marital history. Investigators learned that Dorothy had divorced Overton in 1969 after she learned that, while still married to her, he had secretly married another woman with whom he had a child. At the

INHERITANCE POWDER

The first person to isolate arsenic—dubbed "inheritance powder" for the way it changed certain family fortunes in medieval times—was a Dutch scientist named Johann Metzger. In the 1790s he conducted a string of experiments that showed that if substances containing arsenic were heated and a cold plate held over the vapors, a white layer of arsenious oxide would form on the plate. While this "arsenic mirror" could prove that food had been dosed with arsenic, it could not tell if a body had already absorbed arsenic. For that development, fast-forward a few decades to 1832 when James Marsh, a middle-aged London chemist, was asked to analyze some coffee that a George Bodle of Plumstead had drunk just before his death. Marsh found arsenic present—as he testified to the inquest jury, which returned a verdict of willful murder against Bodle's grandson, John Bodle. Despite this, a trial jury refused to believe Marsh and Bodle was acquitted. (A decade later, Bodle confessed.)

Frustrated by this failure, Marsh focused his attention on the problem of detecting arsenic in the human body. By 1836 he had developed a method of combusting arsenic in such a way that it was unmistakably deposited on cold porcelain. It was similar to Metzger's method, but instead of allowing the vapors to rise up to the cold metal plate—with most of the time Overton had worked at an aerospace company and he had stolen the identity of a coworker to go through the ceremony. He kept up the pretense for 18 months. Every few weeks, one wife would drop him off at the airport as if he were departing on some business trip, and then, a short while later, the other would pick him up from arrivals, looking for all the world as if he was returning home. The scam collapsed when Caroline Hutcheson, the "second" wife, called her husband's place of work and got through to someone whom she had never met before. Ms. Hutcheson got an annulment just before Dorothy Boyer obtained her divorce from Overton.

---

gases escaping into thin air—the whole process took place in a sealed U-shaped tube in which the vapors could only exit via a small nozzle. The suspect material was dropped onto a zinc plate covered with dilute sulfuric acid to produce hydrogen. Any arsenine gas was then heated as it passed along a glass tube, condensing when it reached a cold part of the tube to form the "arsenic mirror." For this outstanding triumph Marsh was awarded a gold medal by the Society of Arts.

But Marsh still wasn't satisfied. He continued refining the test and in 1840 his work finally came to widespread public notice during the trial of Marie Lafarge, a Frenchwoman charged with murdering her husband. The original forensic examination found no trace of arsenic in his body, but the court ordered a new test. The body was exhumed and was found, using Marsh's test, to contain arsenic. This evidence convicted Lafarge, who was sentenced to life imprisonment. The case caused a sensation on both sides of the channel and ensured that Marsh's name became a familiar one to the public. In a refined form, the Marsh test is still in use today.

Marsh was a remarkable chemist with an eclectic mind. He made advances in the design of electromagnetic rotating cylinders and, during his time at the Royal Arsenal in Woolwich, he also invented a percussion cap for naval guns. The man whose greatest legacy was that he discovered how to identify "inheritance powder" died in 1846, at age 51.

Aware by now that they were dealing with someone who had exhibited highly erratic behavioral patterns, investigators decided to review the death of Janet Overton. Although tests on the eyeliner from Overton's library did register traces of selenium, the histological samples retained by the coroner's office were negative. But what struck toxicologist Paul Sedgwick, as he removed Janet's stomach contents from storage, was the distinctive smell of bitter almonds.

Detective novelists have long drawn on the knowledge that the smell of bitter almonds during autopsy is an indicator of the presence of cyanide in the body. Less well known is the fact that the ability to smell hydrogen cyanide is genetic, restricted to only 40 percent of the population. Fortunately, Sedgwick fell into this category. Because homicidal poisoning is exceedingly rare in the United States, unless the medical examiner is specifically checking for some toxic agent during an autopsy, it is easy to overlook. When Sedgwick applied dedicated tests, he found sufficient cyanide in the samples and the stomach contents to warrant an official U-turn. On December 21, 1988, Janet's death certificate was amended to show that she died from acute cyanide intoxication.

One year after the cremation, Overton was brought in for questioning. During the interview, detectives initially kept their knowledge of his tampering record under wraps, as they tapped him for ideas as to who might have poisoned Janet. Overton mentioned that his ambitious wife had made a lot of political enemies over the years: one of them possibly? Then detectives sprang the trap, exposing Overton's tampering background. His response was dramatic. He immediately got up and walked out.

Before leaving, Overton snapped that he had no access to cyanide. However, an acquaintance, Mel Hubbard, who ran a mining operation, admitted that he used cyanide in the extraction of gold and silver from ore, and that Overton frequently visited the cyanide store.

Having established that Overton had the means and the opportunity to poison his wife, detectives went searching for motive. They found it in Overton's own writings, a voluminous diary that he kept in both handwritten and computer form. Overton, a mathematician with a doctorate in psychology, had gone to great lengths to cover his tracks, cod-

A toxicologist, shown here examining some muscle tissue, deals with suspected cases of poisoning. *Colin Cuthbert/Photo Researchers, Inc.*

ing many of his diary entries in Spanish and Russian. The handwritten version showed clear signs of alteration; entries had been whited-out with typing correction fluid, and the page detailing the day of his wife's death had been removed completely. But UV light allowed detectives to read through the whited-out passages, and discover Overton's fury over his wife's infidelity.

It was a similar story with his computer; files had been changed or deleted. This was in the early days of widespread computer usage and Overton, for all his computer smarts, didn't realize that when a file is deleted, only the first letter of its name is changed, telling the computer that this disk space is now available for new data. Until another file overwrites that area, the old file remains intact, and can easily be retrieved. Even when the original file *has* been overwritten, all is not necessarily safe. Modern-day software programs can retrieve almost anything on the disk. In this case, both the hard drive and the 131 disks found in Overton's possession were subjected to a barrage of retrieval software, in the first forensic computer probe in Orange County history.

Joe Enders, a special agent/computer specialist with the Criminal Investigation Division of the Internal Revenue Service, who later testified at Overton's trial, found fragments of files, indicating that Overton had attempted to transfer the contents of his personal diary onto a computer disk. Except that he had run out of space. "He probably got a message that there was not sufficient space on the disk to hold the diary," said Enders. "He must have replaced the disk with a new one, which he probably hid or destroyed."[3] Overton, thinking he had covered

POISON, POISON EVERYWHERE . . .

Although arsenic has generally been the poisoner's weapon of choice, there are hundreds of other lethal toxins in existence. Indeed, most substances—even water—if taken in sufficient quantities have the ability to kill. When Leah Betts, an English teenager, died on November 16, 1995, the tabloid press was quick to blame her death on reports that she had lapsed into a coma four hours after taking an Ecstasy tablet. Although she had taken the illegal drug, an autopsy revealed that it wasn't Ecstasy that killed her; it was the raging thirst that followed. Leah died from drinking too much water. (The medical term is water intoxication.) It is estimated that Leah drank 15 pints of water in 90 minutes. What this tragedy demonstrates is the need for extreme care at all times.

Toxic materials exist in many forms (gaseous, liquid, solid, animal, mineral, and vegetable), and may be ingested, inhaled, or absorbed through the skin. Poisons can either enter the body in a single massive dose, or accumulate over time. It is the latter method that is most commonly employed by the deliberate poisoner; a stealthy erosion of the victim's health to the point where death is both expected and non-suspicious.

his tracks, had actually blundered. Enders knew that while there was no indication of a file on the disk, when someone tries to copy something onto a disk, the computer writes one cluster after another. "If there isn't enough space to copy the entire file, the machine tells the user there's not enough space. It goes back and deletes the file entry in the directory, but leaves all the information it had already written to the disk. So except for the very end of the diary, which there wasn't space for, all the information was still on there."[4]

Hundreds of laboratory hours allowed experts to painstakingly reconstruct Overton's diary, word by word, revealing his innermost thoughts, his profound hatred of Janet. It also provided the ammunition the state needed to charge him with murder.

The following is a list of the most common poisons and their typical symptoms:

Poison	Symptom
Acids (nitric, hydrochloric, sulfuric)	Burns around mouth, lips, nose
Arsenic (metals, mercury, copper, etc.)	Acute, unexplained diarrhea
Atropine (belladonna)	Pupil of eye dilated
Bases (lye, potash, hydroxides)	Burns around mouth, lips, nose
Carbolic acid	Odor of disinfectant
Carbon monoxide	Skin is bright cherry red
Cyanide	Quick death, red skin, odor of almond
Food poisoning	Vomiting, abdominal pain
Metallic compounds	Diarrhea, vomiting, abdominal pain
Nicotine	Convulsion
Opiates	Pupil of eye contracted
Oxalic acid (phosphorous)	Odor of garlic
Sodium fluoride	Convulsion
Strychnine	Convulsion, dark face and neck
Thallium	Hair loss

BIZARRE MISTRIAL

Overton proved to be a champion staller during the preliminary legal proceedings, citing health problems for the delays. One year, two years, three years passed, but finally on April 20, 1992, Overton faced a jury on a charge of murder. Each day before testimony began Overton would theatrically place a lone, white nitroglycerin pill on the defense table before him; a pointed reminder to the jury of his own rumored heart trouble. Overton didn't just give the court a tough time, he was merciless on his own lawyer, Robert Chatterton. So strained did the relationship become, and so vexed was Chatterton over the inability of his client to tell the truth on the stand—or anywhere else, for that matter—that he plunged into a slough of depression. Lawyer frustration with clients is as old as the law itself, but Chatterton was pushed beyond the brink. He suffered a complete mental collapse. "I virtually couldn't get out of my seat in the courtroom," he said later. "I was going through token words [*sic*] just because I was quite overwhelmed at the inability to do anything."[5] Chatterton's disintegration left Superior Court Judge David Carter with no alternative but to declare a mistrial. Overton's delight was obvious, and improved enormously by the decision to free him on $250,000 bail (later reduced to $150,000 by Judge Carter to allow Overton the $100,000 difference to help pay for defense experts.) But Overton's arrogance was unstoppable. Repeated transgressions of his bail conditions led to his being jailed on May 27, 1994, until whenever the second trial began.

That turned out to be March 27, 1995. During the course of the trial, Overton kept up a lively discourse with the packed press gallery. "What they're [the prosecution] taking is one stupid prank of 22 years ago," he lectured the assembled journalists, "and creating this monstrous fact that I've been poisoning people ever since."[6]

Because poisoning is very rare in the United States, prosecutors struggled to find a suitably qualified homegrown expert witness to testify. For this reason, they turned to Dr. Bryan Ballantyne, a British toxicologist with many years' experience of helping the police, to explain the effects of long-term poisoning. He told how Janet Overton's symptoms—nausea, diarrhea, skin lesions, and swollen, discolored feet—echoed those that had afflicted Dorothy Boyer all those years before. Ballantyne attributed Janet Overton's failing health to "metal toxicity,"[7] with selenium the most likely source. The evidence strongly suggested that Overton had been slowly poisoning Janet with selenium for years, and then he stopped, allowing the selenium to evacuate her system before administering the lethal dose of cyanide that was found in the samples.

Overton insisted that the cyanide in Janet's system had originated from her ulcer medication, while his lawyers argued that Janet had not died from cyanide at all, but had rather been a victim of cardiac arrhythmia, an abnormal beating of the heart. The jury was not impressed with either scenario. On May 8, they convicted Overton of first degree murder with the special circumstance of administering poison. This allowed Superior Court Judge Robert R. Fitzgerald to subsequently sentence Overton to life imprisonment without the possibility of parole.

5

The VANPAC
Bomber

Criminals, for the most part, tend to be creatures of habit. They find something that works and stick with it. Serial killers incline toward similar victims; most burglars have their favored method of entry; muggers (or worse) prefer to operate in a familiar geographical area; while thugs with a fondness for illegal firearms seem almost never to discard a weapon, no matter how much its possession might incriminate them. For this lack of imagination, the public should be grateful, because stupidity leads to repetition, and repetition is the criminal's Achilles' heel. It gets him or her caught. Detectives are quick to spot patterns and familiar procedures. Each day they process evidence at crime scenes, and over time they come to recognize the telltale signs that will lead them to a suspect. When memories falter, there is always the computer database to fall back on. A few keystrokes will generally cross-reference a list of similar crimes and culprits. Repetition is one of the most important aspects of evidence evaluation. Indeed, there are times when it provides the only clue available.

On December 16, 1989, Judge Robert S. Vance, 58, received a parcel at his home in exclusive Mountain Brook, Alabama, just outside Birmingham. If the judge thought it was an early Christmas present he was gravely mistaken. As he tore open the package, a pipe bomb inside erupted, hurling a murderous salvo of 80 nails at 3,000 feet per second in all directions, killing Vance and severely injuring his wife, Helen. Vance, only the third federal judge to be assassinated in the 20th century, had

made a lot of enemies in his career, particularly through his strong support for black civil rights—former Alabama governor George Wallace
was a longtime foe of the now-dead jurist—leading many to wonder if
Vance had fallen victim to right-wing extremists.

Two days later, at the Eleventh Circuit Court of Appeals building in
Atlanta, Georgia where Judge Vance had officiated, a mail bomb was
delivered. Fortunately, it was discovered in time and defused safely.

That same day—December 18—at about 5:00 P.M. an identical bomb
killed Robert E. Robinson, a black Savannah, Georgia lawyer, as he sat
at his desk opening the afternoon mail. The blast literally blew him out
of his shoes. Some indication of its strength can be gauged from the fact
that one square metal end plate of the gunpowder-filled pipe bomb was
found embedded in a wall two rooms away.

Twenty-four hours later another bomb was defused at the National
Association for the Advancement of Colored People (NAACP) head-
quarters in Jacksonville, Florida. Several members of the Eleventh Circuit Court also received threatening letters that read:

> JUDGE: AMERICANS FOR A COMPETENT FEDERAL JUDICIAL
> SYSTEM SHALL ASSASSINATE YOU BECAUSE OF THE FEDERAL
> COURTS' CALLOUSED [sic] DISREGARD FOR THE ADMINISTRA-
> TION OF JUSTICE. 010187.

The letters went on to threaten more attacks on black targets, hard-
ening media speculation that these outrages were the work of white
supremacists. But the investigators preferred to concentrate on the
evidence. They saw that the murderous mail deliveries shared several
characteristics: all were packed in brown cardboard boxes wrapped
in brown paper, tied with string, addressed with typed red-and-white
labels, and all had been posted with stamps depicting an American
flag over Yosemite National Park. None of the stamps had been licked,
so there was no chance of obtaining the sender's DNA profile from
any saliva. And further evidence of the bomb maker's meticulousness
could be gauged from the fact that every square inch of the package's
interior had been coated with black enamel paint, to mask any possible
fingerprints or other trace evidence. But the killer had made one serious
blunder; he didn't realize that when bombs explode, large parts of the

bomb itself remain intact. And these particular bombs and fragments would turn out to be very informative indeed.

The VANPAC investigation—so-called because it involved the assassination of Judge *Van*ce with a bomb sent in a mail *pac*kage—was headed by the FBI and their efforts targeted two areas: the bombs, of course, and the letters. Early excitement came with the discovery of a fingerprint on one letter, but anticipation fizzled when it was learned that there was no match in the files. After that, it was a matter of trying to identify the typewriter used to write the letters. Special Agent William Bodziak, a certified document examiner, noticed that all the typed documents displayed a uniform horizontal spacing of the typewritten characters of 2.35 millimeters. This identifying characteristic was traced to a line of typewriters produced by Brother Industries. Further study showed that the typewriter used to type the letters had an irregular number "1" key. At first this was thought to be an individual flaw, but it was later found to be a distinguishing trait of a small range of Brother manual typewriters produced between 1961 and 1962. Immediately a search of government records began, to see whether any documents had been typed on a similar machine.

Elsewhere at the FBI, scientists had their hands full analyzing the bombs. Their construction was highly unusual. Each comprised a steel pipe packed with smokeless powder, with welded flat end plates joined together by a steel rod that ran through the pipe, a feature designed to fractionally delay the explosion and thereby drastically enhance its explosive impact. Nails were tightly packed around this rod, and the device was triggered by a string attached to the packaging. A detonator had been fashioned from a flashbulb filament with distinctive wiring and a ballpoint pen casing. The detonators from the two unexploded bombs contained a green powder identified as a small arms primer manufactured by CCI Industries. Uniquely for their kind, CCI primers had a 2 percent aluminum content. A specialized form of infrared analysis confirmed that the explosive used in the devices was Red Dot double base smokeless powder made by the Hercules Corporation. No doubt about it, whoever designed these bombs was highly skilled; the workmanship was immaculate and deadly.

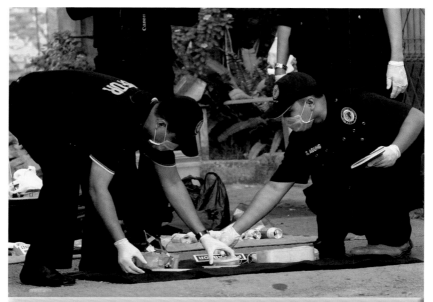

Investigators collect and inspect bombs found in the home of a suspect. Experts involved in the VANPAC investigation were able to link Walter Moody to the bombings partially because the bombs he constructed had a unique "signature." *Adi Weda/epa/Corbis*

A MAJOR BREAKTHROUGH

Meanwhile, the typewriter had thrown up a strong lead; a similar machine had been used to type correspondence in a bitter insurance dispute. When questioned, the author of the letter, Robert O'Ferrell, a used goods dealer who lived in Enterprise, Alabama, vaguely remembered the typewriter in question, and claimed it had been sold to a young woman about a year earlier. On January 22, 1990, with a frenzied media pack in tow, investigators swooped on O'Ferrell's home and property and combed every inch—even to the point of emptying the septic tank—but found nothing to connect him to the crime. Moreover, the poor quality of craftsmanship on household repairs, that agents noted as they searched the property, was light years removed from the painstakingly careful bomb construction. It eventually became clear that O'Ferrell was unconnected to the crimes.

Less well publicized was the fact that, even before this, agents had already achieved a major breakthrough elsewhere. In their attempts to break the impasse, the FBI had circulated pictures of the bombs to no fewer than 217 forensic laboratories nationwide. None reported having seen anything remotely like this bomb before, until Lloyd Erwin, a chemist with Alcohol, Tobacco & Firearms (ATF) in Atlanta studied the photographs. He recalled seeing one just like it back in 1972 in Macon, Georgia. The pipe had been smaller and made out of aluminum alloy, but it had those same distinctive square metal end plates and four bolts going through it. Erwin recalled that the bomb had been intended for an auto dealer who had repossessed a disgruntled customer's car, only for the wife of the man who had constructed the bomb to accidentally detonate the device and severely injure herself. Her husband, Walter Leroy Moody Jr., 37, was convicted of making the bomb and sentenced

THE BATH SCHOOL MASSACRE

Bombs have long been a favored weapon of the politically motivated terrorist, but in 1927 a 55-year-old Michigan farmer named Andrew Kehoe changed forever the detonation dynamic. Like Moody, Kehoe was a world-class grudge bearer. And, again like Moody, he was consumed by a desire for revenge. Kehoe's problems were rooted in money. In May 1927 he learned that the local bank had foreclosed on his farm just outside Bath, Michigan, a small village northeast of Lansing. Rather than look to his own fecklessness—he was a hopelessly inefficient farmer—Kehoe blamed his woes on the Bath School Board, of which he was the treasurer. It was their high taxes, or so his twisted logic reasoned, that made him unable to meet his obligation to the bank. The volcano that had been simmering inside Kehoe for years finally erupted on the morning of May 18.

The first explosion came at 8:45 A.M. when Kehoe's house and barn erupted in a ball of flame. (It was later learned that he had already murdered his wife, Nellie, and dumped her body by the chicken coop.) Next, he drove a mile to the Bath to six years (while Moody was behind bars his wife, Hazel, understandably, divorced him).

Moody had been incensed by the conviction, and after his release had spent 10 years trying to have it overturned, as it doomed his hopes of attending law school. Significantly his final appeal had been thrown out by the Eleventh Circuit Court in Atlanta, just days before Judge Vance received his deadly package.

Moody was a strange person, highly intelligent, dangerously obsessive, and ultra-cautious. When agents descended on his house in Rex, Georgia, they vacuumed every square inch of space in an effort to identify some kind of trace evidence that would link him to the bombs, only to come away empty-handed. Agents next turned their attention to Moody's obviously jittery second wife, Susan, who was 20 years her husband's junior. Under a promise of immunity, she told how Moody

---

Consolidated School. Just after the morning bell a colossal explosion blew the school apart. Thirty-three children lost their lives, together with several teachers. This was no spontaneous outburst of insanity. It later emerged that Kehoe, over several weeks, had been stashing hundreds of pounds of dynamite and **pyrotol** about the school in readiness for this day. This explosion had been detonated by a timer.

Kehoe, apparently, watched the mayhem from the safety of his vehicle. About a half hour after the devastation he beckoned his longtime enemy, school superintendent Emory Huyck, to him. When Huyck drew close, Kehoe turned and, with his rifle, fired once into the backseat of his car. That, too, had been loaded with explosives. The blast killed Kehoe, Huyck and two other men. An eight-year-old second grader named Cleo Claton, who had survived the school explosion, was struck by a piece of shrapnel from this blast and died.

At the end of that dreadful day, 45 people, including the architect of this disaster, lay dead. Another 58 were injured. In the years since there have been many tragedies in the American school system, but none to rival the Bath School Massacre. It remains the bloodiest day in United States' school history.

THE WRITE STUFF

Bombs weren't the only thing that experts studied in the Moody case. They also paid very close attention to the letters that he wrote. Forensic linguistics is a new tool, predicated on the belief that no two people use language in quite the same way. All of us have our idiosyncrasies and preferences, especially when writing, and it is this identifiable individuality that the expert is seeking. One of the most prominent voices in this emerging field belongs to Vassar College literary professor Donald Foster, who operates on the premise that, no matter how we may try to disguise the fact, "Human beings are prisoners of their own language."[1] He first rose to prominence in 1996 when he was asked to identify the anonymous author of the best-selling political novel *Primary Colors*. Within a week, Foster had fingered Joe Klein, a reporter for *Newsday*. Despite some initial denials, Klein eventually admitted responsibility and Foster's reputation soared.

He begins by scouring text databases, searching for similar language habits that will help him "establish the writer's age, gender, ethnicity, level of education, professional training, and ideology."[2] This is complex work. Linguistic clues typically include not just vocabulary, spelling, grammar, and

forced her to go shopping in hardware stores across the southeastern states. On these trips she always wore a scarf, gloves, and sunglasses to disguise her appearance and block her fingerprints. On his instructions she bought steel pipe, rubber gloves, tubing, and black enamel paint. At one store in Georgia, she saw her husband shoplift nails similar to those in the bombs. She also admitted buying the typewriter for her husband, and having later thrown it away.

Corroboration for her story came from that solitary fingerprint. Once, in 1989, she had tried to photocopy the letters in a small store in Florence, Kentucky, only to find the copier was out of paper. When a store employee, Gordon Horton, refilled the copier, he had left his print on the top sheet of paper. It had been his fingerprint that showed on the threatening letter.

syntax, but also word-usage such as slang, professional jargon, regionalisms, even punctuation.

Foster's most successful intervention in the criminal field came, curiously enough, in another explosives case, one that bore remarkable similarities to the Moody case. He was asked by attorneys acting for Theodore Kaczynski, an ex-Harvard professor, to disprove prosecution claims that Kaczynski was the author of the so-called Unabomber Manifesto. For almost two decades, a militant extremist dubbed the Unabomber had waged a campaign of terror that left three dead and 29 seriously injured. In June 1995 the killer had sent a rambling 35,000-word manifesto to the *New York Times* and the *Washington Post*, outlining his grievances. After studying the document closely and comparing it to known samples of Kaczynski's work, Foster had to disappoint the defense—there was absolutely no doubt in his mind that Kaczynski had written the manifesto. Instead, Foster offered his services to the prosecution. Upon hearing this, Kaczynski plea-bargained his way to a sentence that will keep him behind bars forever.

Although Foster's claim that "forensic linguistics is about where DNA evidence was a few years ago"[3] might be stretching the reality, somewhat, this is a forensic discipline destined to grow and grow.

Investigators now cranked up the heat. In Chamblee, Georgia, they found a storage unit rented by Moody, and there uncovered a device constructed from a metal pipe that was similar to the construction of the mail bombs. As the search widened, Paul Sartain, a part-time employee of the Shootin' Iron gun shop in Griffin, Georgia, remembered that in December 1989, two weeks before Judge Vance was killed, Moody had bought "the first and the last keg I've ever sold"[4] of Hercules Red Dot smokeless powder. He said that Moody had also bought 4,000 CCI small pistol primers. Despite the fact that, at the time he made the purchase, Moody had dyed his black hair a dark reddish brown, Sartain had no trouble picking him out at a lineup in May 1990, zeroing in on Moody's "recessed, magnetic eyes."[5]

When FBI agents searched Moody's home on February 13, 1990, they found 17 stamps of the same type as used on the packages, and numerous highlighted newspaper clippings about the investigation of O'Ferrell.

Before the case came to trial, Moody's counsel, Edward Tolley, did everything in his power to get his client to plead insanity. But Moody, who'd been diagnosed with psychiatric problems in 1967, refused point-blank. Tolley wasn't surprised. "He [Moody] sees insanity as an admission of guilt,"[6] he said later.

Owing to the unusual nature of the crimes, all federal judges in the Eleventh Circuit—Alabama, Georgia, and Florida—**recused** themselves, and the defense was granted its request for a change of venue. As a result, Moody was tried in federal court in St. Paul, Minnesota, with proceedings beginning on June 4, 1991. He faced a 71-count indictment and an overwhelming barrage of evidence. Lloyd Erwin, and his fellow ATF forensic chemists, Frank Lee and Terry Byer, took the stand and testified about the construction of the four mail bombs, the 1972 bomb, and the Chamblee device. They were unanimous in their opinion that all the devices had been made by the same person.

INGENIOUS AND UNIQUE

FBI Agent James Thurman said neither he nor anyone else in the labs across the nation had seen a bomb like the one found in Moody's home in 1972 or the four he mailed in 1989. He said each bomb contained threaded rods to seal the pipes and make them more potent. He described the unique detonation method as the "bomber's signature," adding, "I have never observed this specific type of connection before. It's an ingenious design."[7]

Prosecutors also claimed that Moody had carried out a "dress rehearsal"[8] for the pipe bombs, by mailing a tear-gas canister to the Atlanta regional office of the NAACP. This was opened on August 21, 1989, and injured 15 people. The state alleged that Moody had sought to mask his actions by making it appear as though the bombing campaign was racially motivated and carried out by members of the Ku Klux Klan.

Over the strong objections of his attorney, Moody chose to testify. He blamed the killings on a young acquaintance named Gene Wallace, a member of Atlanta's "hippie culture, doing drug dealing and involved in bombing the Pentagon."[9] (No trace of Wallace was ever found, and he is thought to be a figment of Moody's imagination). His performance on the stand, by turns shifty and toweringly arrogant, shattered what little chance he had of acquittal.

On June 28 Moody listened stoically as the word "guilty" was pronounced on him 71 times. At a subsequent sentencing, he was given seven life terms plus 400 years.

But his travails were not over yet. In 1996 the state of Alabama was finally granted its wish and arraigned Moody on two counts of capital murder. At his trial Moody, who fired his lawyers, offered no defense whatsoever, and this time he was sentenced to death. At the time of this writing, Moody is on death row at Holman Correctional Facility.

In 1990 the federal building and courthouse in Birmingham, Alabama, was renamed the Robert Smith Vance Federal Building and Courthouse in memory of the late jurist.

In this case, it was Moody's blinkered refusal to change his *modus operandi* that led to his downfall. It never occurred to him that by making his bombs in so distinctive a fashion, he might just as well have written his name and address on each package. Even so, it still took an eagle-eyed scientist to recognize Moody's handiwork from 17 years previously. Without the intervention of Lloyd Erwin, it is entirely possible that these crimes could have gone unpunished.

6

The False Confession

The confession is a cornerstone of the American judicial system. Some view it as the holy grail of evidence. After all, what can be more compelling for a prosecutor than to stand up in court and say, "Ladies and gentlemen of the jury, I have here the prisoner's signed confession." As evidence goes, it doesn't get much better than that. Once made, a confession is extraordinarily difficult to retract. It clings to the defendant like moss on a rock. Investigators and prosecutors know this, and they also know just how much store a jury puts in an admission of guilt. This is why, in their desperation to deliver what the jury wants, many investigative agencies have overstepped the mark.

At one time, use of the "third-degree" was a common method of refreshing memories and obtaining that all-important confession. But as time passed, and court scrutiny tightened, a new sophistication crept into the equation. Investigators learned that suggestible prisoners could be "coaxed" into phony admissions of guilt. Fortunately, though, the judicial process never stands still. Neither does science. And as both expand they are constantly seeking out new methods of examining evidence.

In the 1980s, a British scientist, Dr. Alec Jeffeys, developed what has become the greatest evidential advance since the advent of fingerprint testimony. The courts—if not all of its practitioners—welcomed DNA profiling with open arms. Here was a tool that could not just convict the guilty, but even more importantly, exonerate the innocent. And it soon got a chance to prove its credentials, by driving a gaping hole through one of the most notorious jailhouse confessions obtained in recent years.

When Susan Tucker, a 44-year-old Department of Agriculture employee, was found strangled inside her Fairlington Villages townhouse in Arlington, Virginia on December 1, 1987—she had been dead for several days—one of the investigating officers called to the gruesome scene was Detective Robert Carrig. A slip-knotted rope was tied around Susan's neck; the free end of the knotted rope had been used to tie her hands behind her back. As he absorbed these details, Carrig felt a chill. Turning to his partner, Detective Joe Horgas, he muttered, "It's Carolyn Hamm all over again."[1]

Almost four years previously, on January 25, 1984, someone broke into the bedroom of Washington-based lawyer Carolyn Hamm at her home at 4921 South 23rd Street, just four blocks away from where this latest murder had occurred. She, too, had been strangled and sexually assaulted, with the killer leaving her suspended from a water pipe, with a noose around her neck.

On that occasion a suspect had been arrested inside of two weeks. David Vasquez, a 37-year-old fast-food restaurant employee, who worked about two blocks from where Hamm lived, had been seen by one of Hamm's neighbors at about the time the murder occurred. Carrig remembered the case so vividly because he had been one of the officers who'd interviewed the mentally subnormal Vasquez. Over the course of three long, arduous interviews, Vasquez revealed details of the crime that only the killer and the police could know. A firm belief took hold with prosecutors that Vasquez was the murderer, especially when he confessed.

MIRANDA BLUNDER

But the detectives had been too aggressive, and they'd cut corners. Although Vasquez was charged with capital murder, a judge ruled that two of Vasquez's statements were inadmissible because the prisoner had not been read his **Miranda rights**. This led to some legal horse-trading. The state offered a deal; if Vasquez agreed to plead guilty to second-degree homicide, he would be spared the death penalty. Vasquez, terrified out of his wits by the prospect of a date with the electric chair, had jumped at the offer.

On February 4, 1985, Vasquez was imprisoned for 35 years. At his brief trial, excerpts from his one admissible statement were read. In this Vasquez described the "horrible dreams"[2] he had suffered since the crimes. In one affidavit another detective, N. E. Tyler, said that Vasquez told him that he "formulated the method used to kill Miss Hamm from reading books on bondage and sadomasochism."[3]

Three years on and Detective Carrig was decidedly thoughtful. At no time had Vasquez mentioned anything about an accomplice, but this latest murder—with its uncanny similarities to the strangling of

THE THIRD DEGREE

The term "third degree" is thought to derive from **Freemasonry** where a candidate receives the third or highest degree, that of master mason, upon passing an intensive test. Dating from the 1770s, the phrase was transferred to other kinds of interrogation in the late 1800s. By 1902 the third degree was part of the fabric of police life right across America. As the outrages became more flagrant and more brutal, newspapers such as the *New York Times* began calls for its abolition.

The "third degree" took many forms. In its original incarnation, the prisoner was simply kept in solitary in a darkened cell for hours, sometimes days, at a time. Sensory deprivation can play cruel tricks on the human mind. But some prisoners were too mentally strong and it was for them that the notorious "sweatbox" was developed. This was a special room, usually in a little visited part of the jailhouse, about six feet square and eight feet high. Thick blankets were draped across the walls and ceilings to keep light out and heat in. In summer the temperatures could soar to well over 100 degrees. The prisoner was not allowed any visitors. His only human contact was a guard, who kept prompting the prisoner to confess. After several days of this kind of treatment, most prisoners broke and confessed to whatever they were told.

Those hardy souls that still held out passed on to the next level of torture: "salting the bread." As the name implies,

Carolyn Hamm—raised that very possibility. It was a chilling prospect. Was there a serial killer on the loose in Washington, D.C.?

Just over 100 miles to the south, detectives in Richmond, Virginia, were also coming to terms with that same grim reality. A spate of murders had broken out on that city's south side, beginning on September 18, 1987, when Debbie Dudley Davis, 35, was murdered in her Westover Hills apartment. Two weeks later, just a few streets away, Marcel Sleg came home to find his wife, Dr. Susan Hellams, 32, a neurosurgery resident at the Medical College of Virginia Hospitals, stuffed into a

---

prisoners were fed a lone diet of bread that had been heavily salted. Then water was withheld. This trapped the prisoner in a terrible quandary; assuage the pangs of hunger or aggravate a raging thirst?

The notorious Tombs Prison in New York had probably the most sophisticated third degree operation. The "dark cell,"[4] as it was known, was situated on one of the upper tiers. Made entirely of iron and stone, it had a door whose massive iron bars were covered with screens to prevent the slightest penetration of light. A tiny, darkened sliver was the only admittance for air. After a few hours in this hellhole, even the toughest prisoner was ready to admit to anything.

Of course, many police forces scoffed at such sophistication. They simply took a length of rubber hose and beat the prisoner about the body until the required words began flowing. How many people were imprisoned because of false jailhouse confessions is impossible to calculate, but the practice was so widespread that even the most conservative estimate would put the number in the thousands.

It is unlikely that the use of the third degree will ever be eliminated entirely. Even the highest government agencies are not immune, with reports in 2007 that the U.S. Department of Justice had authorized a variant of the third degree—known as **waterboarding**—on Al-Qaeda and Taliban detainees around the world.

bedroom closet. She too had been raped and strangled. On November 22, the man dubbed the "Southside Strangler" struck again, this time killing 15-year-old student Diane Cho at her home in a Chesterfield County apartment complex. Also found at the Cho crime scene was a single hair that appeared to be Negroid in origin. The family confirmed that they had never had any African-American visitors, so it was reasonable to assume that this came from the killer.

Like the Arlington victims, each woman had been attacked in her own bedroom, each had her hands tied behind her back, each had been raped, and each had been strangled with a rope. The only link between the victims that investigators could find was that all three regularly frequented Cloverleaf Mall, a shopping center in Chesterfield County. Debbie Dudley Davis worked at a bookstore in the mall; Susan Hellams bought books at this store; while Diane Cho was a regular visitor. This raised the possibility that the killer was using the mall to select his victims.

Oblivious to the murderous events in Richmond—because the crimes occurred in different jurisdictions, neither law enforcement agency made the connection between the two murder sprees—Arlington detectives pursued their belief that the Hamm and Tucker cases were related, a possibility that increased significantly when forensic scientist Deanne Dabbs analyzed four samples of bodily fluids found on Susan Tucker's bedding. These turned out to be type O with a particular enzyme profile that matched just 13 percent of the population—including the killer of Caroline Hamm.

All of this only strengthened the conviction of detectives in Arlington that Vasquez must have had an accomplice. They began trawling through old crime cases looking for a pattern, anything that might give them a name. Then someone recalled that back in 1983 an uncaught rapist had terrorized the neighborhood where Susan Tucker was murdered, using an identical means of incapacitating his victims. Was it possible that the rapist had now graduated to murder? This sparked a new round of inquiries. Detective Joe Horgas did some digging and spoke to another officer who remembered that one of the 1983 rape victims had been stuffed into the trunk of a car and then the car had been set alight. There was something about this case that set Horgas thinking. He then recalled that back in 1970 a 10 year old—"All I could remember was [the name] Timmy"[5]—had set a fire. When Horgas began jogging neighborhood memories, tongues loosened and soon he had the name he was looking for—Timothy Wilson Spencer.

Spencer was a 25-year-old loner, with a jarringly defensive attitude that no one seemed able to penetrate. At age 10, following his arrest for starting the fire, he had been diagnosed as emotionally disturbed and he'd spent most of his adulthood proving the accuracy of that diagnosis. In terms of personality, he fit the profile of the attacker. But there was just one problem: Spencer was already behind bars. At the end of January 1984, shortly after the Hamm killing, he had been arrested on a burglary charge, found guilty and jailed. It looked like another dead end, until a closer check of the prison inmate records in Virginia showed that Spencer had become eligible for a halfway house scheme, whereby he was allowed out of prison on a temporary basis, prior to making his application for full parole.

By now law enforcement agencies in Richmond and Arlington were coordinating efforts, and what really set investigative pulses racing was the realization that the privately run halfway house where Spencer was registered, the OAR Hospitality House at 1500 Porter Street in south Richmond, was adjacent to the area where the latest killing binge had occurred. Moreover, at the time of Susan Tucker's murder, Spencer had been granted a furlough to visit his mother who lived in Arlington, just seven blocks away from Susan Tucker's townhouse. For the first time a connection had been made between the Arlington killings and those in Richmond.

A coordinated investigation led to Spencer being placed under discreet round-the-clock surveillance. On the night of January 9, 1988, a detective tailed Spencer to the Cloverleaf Mall. He spent about half an hour there, just wandering around, and then left. When arrested on January 20 at the halfway house, Spencer vehemently denied having ever visited the Cloverleaf Mall. All of his clothing was taken to the crime lab for testing. A green camouflage jacket that he wore regularly, when combed for trace evidence, yielded several glass fragments. Glass refraction analysis of these fragments—achieved by directing light from several different points on the spectrum through the particles to see how the sample bent the beam, then plotting these results on a graph—showed that these fragments matched the optical properties of Tucker's broken basement window. Only 2 percent of glass examined at the state laboratory had the same optical characteristics. In isolation this would not have been sufficient to guarantee a conviction, but the investigators had a new tool to work with, and this one was revolutionary.

THE FOUNDER OF DNA FINGERPRINTING

At 9 o'clock on the morning of September 15, 1984, a 34-year-old British scientist, Dr. Alec Jeffreys, changed the course of crime-fighting history. Jeffreys, a research fellow at Leicester University's Lister Institute, had just returned to his laboratory where, over the weekend, he had left some x-ray film in a developing tank. Now, as he held the film aloft and saw the distinctive display of stutter sequences, a single thought raced through his mind: "My God what have we got here!"[6] Almost by accident he'd stumbled across a way of establishing a human's genetic identification. (Twenty-five years on, and that first DNA film still hangs on his office wall.) By that afternoon, he and the rest of his team had named the discovery "DNA fingerprinting."

Jeffreys first became fascinated with genetics while still a postgraduate student at Oxford University. At the core of his work was a belief that by comparing two people's DNA it would be possible to identify an almost unlimited number of genetic differences. Jeffreys knew that the short chunks of DNA that vary most between individuals—called "minisatellites"—are repeated over and over again. But this created a problem: How could these sequences be located?

Jeffreys wrestled with this conundrum as he continued his studies in Holland. In 1977 he returned to England to take up a post as lecturer in genetics at the University of Leicester. More years of frustration followed, and then came his eureka moment.

THE DNA REVOLUTION

In 1984 a British scientist named Dr. Alec Jeffreys, had made a landmark discovery in forensic science. Even though DNA—the genetic code that determines every aspect of our physical appearance—had been studied for decades, it was Jeffreys who perfected the means whereby identifiable genetic markers could be developed on an x-ray film as a kind of

The first practical application of DNA fingerprinting came with the settlement of a British immigration dispute. It was Jeffreys's technology that allowed a Ghanaian woman and her son to be reunited, after he had established their biological connection beyond all reasonable doubt.

Although Jeffreys was quick to realize the forensic implications of DNA fingerprinting, he also recognized its pitfalls. In the early days a lot of good quality DNA was required to obtain a good DNA fingerprint, and all too often at crime scenes there was insufficient biological evidence to attempt a match with the DNA of a suspect. Also, old DNA can degrade, leading to problems of interpretation.

In 1985 Jeffreys and his team developed a technology that overcame these limitations. Called DNA profiling, it enabled them to isolate individual mini-satellites and produce a pattern on x-ray film requiring just two bands per individual: one from the person's mother and one from their father. Simpler to read and interpret, DNA profiles can also be stored on a computer database. Most significant of all, they can be obtained from much smaller samples.

After his technique led to the conviction of serial murderer, Colin Pitchfork, the quiet academic from Leicester University became an international celebrity. In 1994 he was knighted for his services to science and technology. Since that time Sir Alec Jeffreys has continued his work at Leicester University, in the knowledge that his discovery revolutionized the business of crime solving in every corner of the globe.

British geneticist, Dr. Alec Jeffreys developed the technique of DNA fingerprinting, which is used worldwide in criminal investigations. *Corbin O'Grady Studio/Photo Researchers, Inc.*

bar code and then compared with other specimens. On November 21, 1986, in England, history was made when DNA profiling freed a young man suspected of double murder. Fourteen months later, on January 22, 1988, the real killer, Colin Pitchfork, made his own mark in the crime annals by becoming the first murderer in the world to be convicted through the use of DNA testimony.

Jeffreys's revolutionary discovery had made global headlines. And prosecutors in Virginia were convinced that this groundbreaking technology held the key to convicting a savage serial killer. Spencer's defense team fought like demons to prevent their client from having to provide samples of blood, hair, and saliva, but the courts struck down all of their objections. Samples from the various crime scenes and a test sample from Spencer were sent to Lifecodes, a New York-based company that was at the cutting edge of DNA technology in the United States. This wasn't the first DNA case in America. Florida had already indicated its willingness to accept DNA testimony in the case of Tommie Lee Andrews—on February 5, 1988, Andrews was sentenced to 115 years for rape—so there was a precedent for the use of DNA typing. When Lifecodes did the tests their results were unequivocal. Spencer was judged to be the person who had murdered Susan Tucker and Debbie Davis, with a certainty put at one in 135 million.

Even more significantly, Spencer's DNA also branded him—and not David Vasquez—as the killer of Caroline Hamm. As it soon became apparent that no vestige of a link existed between Spencer and David Vasquez, and because the FBI's Behavioral Unit believed that the highly distinctive *modus operandi* in all five murders, including the Hamm case, was strongly indicative of a single killer, an immediate appeal was lodged on behalf of Vasquez.

On July 12, 1988, Spencer stood trial for the murder of Susan Tucker. Lisa Bennett, who performed the genetic testing at Lifecodes, used an overhead projector to show the jury how molecules of DNA in Spencer's blood matched genetic characteristics from samples recovered at the crime scene. After a trial lasting just three days, Spencer was convicted of murder and later sentenced to death.

At times the wheels of justice grind with unfathomable slowness, and all this time David Vasquez remained behind bars. On October 11, 1988, Arlington Commonwealth's Attorney Helen F. Fahey finally announced that she was recommending that David Vasquez be pardoned. She stated that she did not "believe he was involved"[7] in the slaying of Carolyn Jean Hamm. Even this was not enough to win freedom for Vasquez. So slowly did the bureaucratic wheels creak into action, that Vasquez was still behind bars when Spencer was given a second death sentence, this time on November 2 1988, for the murder of Debbie Dudley Davis.

Not until January 4, 1989, did Vasquez get the news he was waiting for. Virginia Governor Gerald L. Bailes announced that he was granting a complete pardon and Vasquez was released. The following year, the state Senate assessed Vasquez's ordeal as worth $1,000 per month for 19 years, awarding him a total of $228,000 for five years in prison. His ordeal demonstrated vividly just how lethal a false confession can be.

In the meantime, on January 20, 1989, Spencer had received a third death sentence, this time for killing Susan Hellams. In all of the trials,

DNA evidence was critical. Without it Spencer would have walked free. There was, understandably, little appetite for Spencer's appeal process and on April 27, 1994, he went to the electric chair, the first killer in the United States to be executed through the use of DNA evidence.

In a quite remarkable coincidence, the first American murder case to feature DNA profiling had exactly mirrored its groundbreaking British forerunner: Not only had the new technique convicted the guilty party, it had also exonerated a man who was wholly innocent. Without the miracle of DNA profiling, Vasquez's false confession—the product of a suggestible mind overwhelmed by stronger personalities—would never have come to light and he would still be serving time for a crime he didn't commit. Little wonder then, that DNA is regarded as the greatest breakthrough in forensic science since the introduction of fingerprinting.

Eyewitness and Expert Testimony

The human memory is a notoriously fallible instrument. Show two eye-witnesses the same scene, tell them to go away, come back one month later, and then ask them to recall what they saw. Chances are they will give two versions of events that, while broadly similar, will contain significant differences. Constant retellings only tend to widen these divergences. These very human failings can cause genuine problems for the judicial process, because memory is such an important component of any trial.

In recent years this problem has been exacerbated by the introduction of testimony that has flirted with the outer boundaries of human recall. This tends to fall into one of two categories. The first is so-called repressed memory, where a person claims to suddenly recall an incident, often a traumatic one, that has been buried in the psyche for many years. This is highly contentious and has fared poorly in the courtroom. Too many examples have surfaced of patients being prompted, through the use of hypnosis or other techniques, to reveal disturbing allegations that are more the product of the therapist's skillful manipulation than the witness's memory. Next, is what psychologists term "false memory syndrome." This is a condition in which a person's identity and personal relationships are strongly influenced by a false but strongly believed memory of a traumatic experience, such as alleged sexual abuse by a parent or other relative or abduction by alien beings.

It was this syndrome that came under the judicial microscope in Phoenix, Arizona, in 1995, when a jury listened to the testimony of a woman who had kept a terrible secret buried for almost three decades. What the jury had to decide was whether they were listening to the ramblings of a dangerous fantasist, or the honest testimony of a woman who had finally broken the shackles of fear.

On September 19, 1966, a Phoenix office worker named Celia Molina phoned the local police. She was worried because her colleague, DiAnne Keidel, normally so punctual, had not showed up for work, nor had she called to explain her absence. Ms. Molina explained to the officer that DiAnne was getting a divorce and had "expressed fear that

BRAIN FINGERPRINTING

One of the newest and most controversial forensic tools, brain fingerprinting is predicated on the belief that the brain itself can be accessed much like a computer hard drive to retrieve data stored there. The forensic theory of brain fingerprinting works like this: When someone commits a crime, they can't erase the memory of that crime; it stays with them, logged in the brain. Ordinarily, this knowledge remains buried. What brain fingerprinting provides is a window into someone's past visual experience.

A typical brain fingerprinting test requires the subject to don a headband equipped with sensors, and then sit in front of a computer video display unit (VDU). A series of words or pictures pertaining to the crime in question is then shown on the VDU, together with other, irrelevant words or pictures. As the exhibits flash by, the subject's electrical brain activity is monitored by the sensors and recorded by a sophisticated computer program.

The intention is to generate a specific brain-wave response called a MERMER (Memory And Encoding Related Multifaceted Electroencephalographic Response). This occurs when the brain processes noteworthy information that it recognizes. Contained within the MERMER is a scientifically established brain response known as a P300, and it is this that the examiner is focusing on. P300 is a specific electrical brain wave, activated when a person sees a familiar object.

her husband may harm her."[1] It had been a bad marriage littered with extramarital affairs on both sides.

DiAnne had been married before and had a toddler, Karen (known as Susie), by her first husband, from whom she was divorced. In 1956 she had married Lyle Eugene Keidel in their native Peoria, Illinois, and four years later the couple moved to Arizona, where he found work, first as a machinist and then as a self-employed building contractor. But it was not a happy transition. Soon the marriage went into freefall. Both DiAnne and Gene were heavy drinkers and both had violent tempers.

If a person looks at random pictures of weapons, without activating a P300 wave, in all likelihood these objects are unknown to him. But if a suspected killer is shown a murder weapon and a P300 wave is generated, then, according to proponents of brain fingerprinting, that indicates prior knowledge of the weapon. No questions are asked and no answers are given during a brain fingerprinting test; it is a purely visual experience.

There are drawbacks. For the P300 wave to be truly effective, the examiner must demonstrate that the suspect hadn't seen the item in some other innocuous way, such as in media accounts or by being a bystander. Also, brain fingerprinting relies on utter compliance from the subject. Brain-wave data can be obtained only if a person sits reasonably still and looks at the VDU. Anyone seeking to skew the results would only have to act in an agitated fashion to render the test useless.

Despite lavish claims made for its success rate in detecting stored memory, thus far brain fingerprinting has received a cool response from American courts. Its allies lie mostly in the field of national security. The FBI, appalled by the ease with which super spies Aldrich Ames and Donald Hansen repeatedly hoodwinked polygraph experts over several years, has allegedly sunk millions into the new technology. Other agencies such as the CIA are also rumored to be exploring its uses.

Oftentimes, DiAnne had to wear heavy makeup to work, to cover the facial bruises that Gene had inflicted on her. But she gave as good as she got. Once she had bitten Gene so badly that he required hospital treatment. That had been just a few months previously, in the summer of 1966. And now she had vanished.

As it happened, the missing 31 year old's estranged husband had already reported DiAnne's disappearance, saying he'd last seen her the previous Friday. According to Keidel, he and DiAnne had gone to dinner at Taco Bell with the children, and then they had dropped the children off at home about 9:00 P.M. After finalizing details of their upcoming divorce, the couple went out drinking. As the night wore on, Keidel said, DiAnne made numerous phone calls, one of which seemed to upset her. Shortly after this she asked Keidel if she could borrow his car for the remainder of the night and he'd agreed. They had left the West Phoenix bar at around 11:15 P.M., after which DiAnne had dropped Keidel off at his father's house, where he was living temporarily. Keidel's father confirmed that his daughter-in-law had called at the house, then left alone in Gene's car.

Later that night, Keidel said, he'd phoned 12-year-old Susie at the family home in the 4200 block of West Citrus Way, to check if DiAnne had arrived home safely. When told that there was no sign of her, he'd walked the mile to his former residence to babysit. He said he fell asleep on a couch at about 3:00 A.M. Two and a half hours later, when he awoke, his car was in the drive, DiAnne's purse and keys were in the house, but there was no sign of her.

Police did some digging and discovered that, after leaving Gene, DiAnne had gone to a bar where she met another man. When interviewed, Bob Marlin couldn't shed any light on the mystery. It was just as well that the police had contacted him so promptly, because, in a bizarre twist of fate, less than 48 hours later, Marlin dropped dead from a heart attack.

Meanwhile, one day after his wife's disappearance, Gene moved back permanently into the house on Citrus Way, a strong indication that he wasn't expecting DiAnne to return anytime soon. One week later, what had already been a decidedly tepid missing person inquiry was quietly shelved.

To the outside world, life at Citrus Way appeared to be settling into some kind of normality when, just before midnight on January 9, 1967, tragedy struck. The house was suddenly engulfed in flames. Firefighters who rushed to the scene found two sisters, Susie, 12, and Kelly, eight, dead. Susie had given her life, using her own body to shield that of her five-year-old half-sister, Lori, who was dragged out alive. The only brother, Greg, nine, had managed to jump from his bedroom window. He also survived. Lori was horribly burnt over more than 50 percent of her body and would spend the next six months in hospital.

Gene, who'd been at a local laundromat at the time of the fire, had come running when he heard the wailing sirens. Firefighters noticed that he stank of alcohol and was slurring his words. Nor did he stick around at the hospital to see how Lori was getting along. Instead, within four hours of the disaster, he drove to the home of his latest girlfriend and jumped right into bed with her. The tragedy made headlines across Arizona and even in the Keidels' home state of Illinois. But if DiAnne Keidel read the horrifying accounts, they failed to flush her out of hiding, and Gene was left to bring up what remained of his shattered family alone.

CRIME SCENE CALLOUSNESS

Some firefighters who'd battled the blaze were suspicious about its startling intensity and repulsed by Keidel's stomach-churning nonchalance as two of his children lay dead on the front lawn. Despite these misgivings, a coroner's inquest concluded that the fire had started accidentally. An aluminum pot on the stove had overheated and exploded, firing particles of red-hot metal onto nearby curtains and igniting them. If Keidel was grief stricken it didn't show, and it didn't extend to providing headstones for his two deceased daughters. Both were buried in unmarked graves.

There the story remained for over a quarter of a century. Until June 9, 1993, when Lori Romaneck, as she was now named, picked up the phone book and began thumbing through. She finally found the number she was looking for. After a few moments more spent agonizing, her hand reached for the telephone. "Phoenix police? Hey, I need to speak to someone about a homicide. A very old homicide. Can I please come by?"[2] It had taken 27 years; now Lori was ready to unburden her soul.

That same day Lori did indeed go to the station, and what she had to say sent shockwaves through the police department. On the night of her mother's disappearance, Lori said, she and Susie had been awakened by the sound of their parents fighting. The two terrified children had cringed on an upstairs landing as their father, enraged by DiAnne's promiscuity, battered his wife mercilessly. "He was calling her a tramp and a whore,"[3] Romaneck said. Finally, DiAnne slid unconscious to the ground at his feet. At this point, Keidel, towering over his stricken wife, happened to look up and saw his two daughters. He never said a word.

That same night, unaware that his every move was being observed by his two daughters, Keidel dug a grave for his wife's lifeless body, next to the backyard swimming pool. Calling on his skills as a building contractor, three days later he buried his misdeeds beneath a thick layer of concrete.

Five-year-old Lori was confused. She likened her mother's disappearance to the hibernation of her pet tortoise, Touche, who each winter would hide out, digging a hole beneath a sandbox and reappearing several months later. Except her mother never showed up again. It wasn't until a year later, when a neighboring soldier killed in Vietnam was brought home in a casket that she began to understand the meaning of death and with it the realization that her mom would never be coming home.

Over the next few years, Lori grew used to regular beatings from her father. He would suddenly erupt into paroxysms of rage and paddle her with a wooden spoon for no reason whatsoever. All the while her terror multiplied. The first chance she got, she moved away. Shortly after this, in 1980, Keidel sold the house on Citrus Way, confident that by now his secret was safe and that Lori would never breathe a word of what she had seen. But he was wrong.

On hearing Lori's story, the Phoenix police were, at first, deeply skeptical. Who could trust the memory of a five-year-old, especially after an interval of almost three decades? But Lori wouldn't quit, and after 15 months of badgering the Phoenix Police Department finally agreed to act. Since the house on Citrus Way had changed hands, there was an

A forensic officer uses ground-penetrating radar (GPR) to search for buried evidence. GPR led investigators to the body of DiAnne Keidel, providing the basis for the prosecution of her husband, Gene Keidel. *Louise Murray/Photo Researchers, Inc.*

understandable reluctance to dig up the entire backyard. To overcome this problem, the police contacted NecroSearch International.

NecroSearch is a nonprofit organization open for membership by invitation only. Its members are largely drawn from the laboratories of Colorado universities, scientists who volunteer their time and their specialties—such as **anthropology**, **botany**, **entomology** and **geophysics**, to find the hidden burial sites of murder victims. They step in whenever a law enforcement agency asks for their help. Since its formation in 1989, NecroSearch has aided investigations in 27 states, and been consulted by police in several foreign countries.

On this occasion it was geophysicist G. Clark Davenport, a longtime NecroSearch team-member, who flew to Phoenix. He went armed with a ground-penetrating radar (GPR) device. GPR operates by transmitting pulses of ultra high frequency radio waves down into the ground

THE WIZARD OF BERKELEY

No one in America in the early 20th century contributed more to the proper processing of evidence than Edward O. Heinrich, a chemist at the University of California. Heinrich—known as the "Wizard of Berkeley" for the way he managed to solve countless crimes—almost single-handedly established the reputation of the expert witness in the American courtroom.

Unlike many so-called experts of the time, Heinrich made no attempt to talk down to the jury or blind them with scientific jargon. He kept his testimony simple. Juries appreciated this directness as much as they admired his jaw-dropping scientific talents in such areas as microscopy, ballistics, and handwriting analysis.

It was his powers of deduction that made him a legend. His greatest triumph came in 1923 after a train had been robbed in Oregon. Heinrich was sent the only clues; a detonator, a Colt revolver, and a pair of blue dungarees. From these items he was able to provide investigators with a detailed description of their quarry: a left-handed lumberjack from the Pacific Northwest; someone with light brown hair, who rolled his own cigarettes and was careful of his appearance. He was five feet ten, about 165 pounds, and in his early 20s.

Heinrich explained. Because the left-side pockets of the dungarees were more heavily worn than those on the right, it followed that the wearer was left-handed. Chips of Douglas fir—common to the Pacific Northwest—were found in the right through a transducer or antenna. The transmitted energy is reflected from various buried objects or different earth materials, bounced back up through an antenna and then stored in the digital control unit. Davenport was met by Sgt. Mike Torres of the Phoenix Police Department, who escorted him to the backyard. Using the GPR, Davenport scanned the entire backyard and, at a depth of three feet, identified an area of unusual ground disturbance that measured approximately six feet by

pocket, such as might be gathered by a left-handed lumberjack standing with that side nearest the tree. Shreds of loose tobacco in both pockets were an obvious indicator of smoking preference. Simply measuring the overalls gave Heinrich an approximation of the owner's build and height, while a pocket seam yielded several neatly cut fingernail parings, somewhat incongruous for a lumberjack unless he was fastidious about his appearance. The strong pigmentation of a strand of light brown hair, clinging to one button, pointed to someone in their early 20s.

It took just over three years to bring the train robbers to justice. They were a gang known as the D'Autremont Brothers. Sure enough, Roy D'Autremont, age 23 at the time of the robbery, was found to be a left-handed, medium build lumberjack, vain about his appearance, who rolled his own cigarettes.

As Heinrich's reputation grew, he traveled across America, even to Europe, as a consultant. He once reduced his crime-fighting philosophy to five basic questions. "Precisely what happened? Precisely when did it happen? Precisely where did it happen? Why did it happen? Who did it?" These principles guided Heinrich through more than 1,000 cases of every description, criminal and civil.

Heinrich died in 1953. He will be remembered as a powerful force in revolutionizing American police methods, and as a pathfinder who helped change the art of crime detection into a science. But mostly he will be remembered for the brilliance of his intuition. That was peerless.

two feet—right where Lori claimed her mother was buried. When the police broke through the concrete patio, 10 inches down they unearthed a human skull, then a full skeleton. Knotted tightly around the neck was a pair of nylon stockings.

Torres was ecstatic. "We had an idea where it [the body] might be, but the machine pinpointed it and it was right there,"[4] he said later. This way, Davenport saved police the trouble and expense of digging up the entire backyard.

It was a remarkable discovery, but was it the body of DiAnne Keidel?

NAMING THE CORPSE

Forensic anthropologists confirmed that the skeleton was that of a white woman, around five feet four inches tall, who, judging from the pelvic bones, had had at least two children and was aged between 20 and 40 at the time of death—all details consistent with DiAnne Keidel. Also consistent was the discovery in the grave of part of a blue zipper. Lori remembered that her mother had been wearing a blue dress on the night of her disappearance.

Bacterial depredation had eliminated any hope of DNA testing. Even the tooth pulp—often a rich source of DNA material—was too badly damaged to test. Another setback came with news that DiAnne's dentist no longer practiced, and that her dental records had been destroyed, thus blocking off that avenue of identification.

There was something else, however, that might indicate how long the body had been buried. A tree root had grown through the skull, and by examining a section of this root, **dendrochronologist** Thomas Harlan at the University of Arizona, judged it to be 15 years old. This meant that the body had to have been in the ground prior to 1979. All that was left was for anthropologist Dr. Laura Fulginiti to perform a skull and photo superimposition, and there could be no doubt that these were the mortal remains of DiAnne Keidel.

On September 15, 1994—three days before the 28th anniversary of the slaying—Keidel was arrested and charged with first-degree murder. That same month the Phoenix Fire Department assigned two officers to reinvestigate the fatal 1967 house blaze. Two months later they concluded

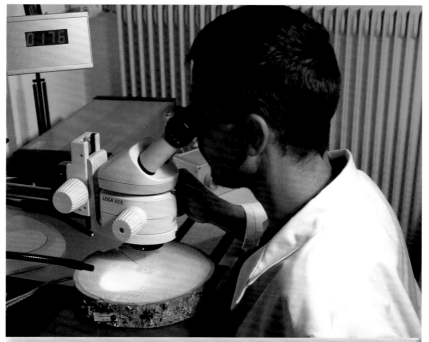

A dendrochronologist uses a microscope to determine the age of a tree. Such analysis was useful in determining how long the body of DiAnne Keidel had been buried. *Mauro Fermariello/Photo Researchers, Inc.*

that the fire had been a case of arson, not an accident. But there was insufficient evidence to pursue a prosecution

Gene Keidel had evaded justice for almost 30 years, and now everything hinged on the jury believing the memory of a five-year-old girl. "In spite of my fears," Lori said, "I decided that I'd rather be dead than to keep the secret."[5] The fact that Lori's memory wasn't repressed—recovered years later only as the result of some new trauma—almost certainly added to her credibility in the view of Tom Hoopes, a criminal defense attorney and former prosecutor. "I don't think the general public finds 'repressed memories' credible,"[6] he said.

Lori's remarkable story, compellingly told and backed up by solid, tangible evidence, made a big impact on the jury. As did the testimony of Keidel's second wife, who recounted how he became nervous when he learned that the new tenants of their former home were doing some backyard renovation work.

When Keidel took the stand he attempted to put his long-dead first wife on trial, blackening her name and reputation with a series of vile claims that DiAnne's brother, Butch Kidder, described as "utter lies."[7] It availed him nothing. On April 17, 1995, now aged 58, Keidel was convicted of first-degree murder. Because the death penalty was not in force in Arizona at the time of the killing, Keidel avoided a date with the gas chamber and was given a maximum sentence of life imprisonment without the possibility of parole.

8

The Random Killer

Crime never stands still. Whether for financial gain or merely malevolent intent, criminals are forever finding new ways to extend their theater of operations. This means that the investigator is always playing catch-up. And this can make the harvesting and processing of evidence hugely difficult.

A new and especially dangerous escalation of criminal activity began on September 29, 1982, when, over a three-day period, seven people in the Chicago area died after taking Extra Strength Tylenol that had been laced with cyanide. Never before had law enforcement agencies had to investigate such a sprawling murder crime scene. The victims were unconnected and the evidence was literally all over town. Three members of the same family were stricken in Arlington Heights; another victim lived a few miles away in Elk Grove Village; the next came from Elmhurst; while the final victim resided in the west Chicago suburb of Winfield. Having to process a crime scene with a radius of 23 miles proved to be a logistical nightmare. Gradually, though, a pattern emerged. As the tainted bottles originated from different factories, it was reasonable to exclude manufacturing sabotage as the cause of the outrage. This meant that someone had toured local supermarkets and drug stores, spiking bottles of Extra Strength Tylenol indiscriminately. Stores were cleared of the offending items (besides the five bottles that caused death, another three tainted bottles were discovered.)

There seemed to be no clear-cut motive for the crime, although a Boston man, James Lewis, was arrested after a letter was delivered to Johnson & Johnson, the manufacturers of Extra Strength Tylenol, demanding $1 million "to stop the killings."[1] On June 15, 1984, Lewis was sentenced to 10 years for extortion, but there was never enough evidence to connect Lewis with the killings and, to date, no charges have ever been filed regarding the Tylenol murders. Over the course of six weeks, more than 1 million capsules were tested. This was evidence processing on an unprecedented scale. As a result of these crimes, more stringent regulations were introduced to avoid product tampering, and in 1983 the Federal Anti-Tampering Act was passed, making it a federal crime to tamper with products or to make false claims of tampering. Oddly enough, the first person to be charged under this act was no urban terrorist or grudge-bearing ex-employee, but rather someone whose motives were rooted in something far more traditional—a craving for money.

As Sue Snow, a 40-year-old bank manager in the Seattle suburb of Auburn, readied herself for work on the morning of June 11, 1986, she suddenly collapsed in her bathroom. Paramedics summoned to the scene found Mrs. Snow semiconscious, unresponsive and gasping for breath. Later that morning she died in the hospital. Doctors were puzzled. The symptoms suggested either an aneurysm or drug overdose, but neither seemed probable because there was no evidence of internal bleeding, and Mrs. Snow was the kind of woman who restricted her drug use to the occasional painkiller. Coincidentally, earlier that morning, to combat a nagging headache, she had taken two Extra Strength Excedrin capsules.

During the autopsy, an assistant detected a faint odor of bitter almonds emanating from the body, a recognized symptom of recently ingested cyanide. A laboratory test came back positive. Family members were vehement in their insistence that Sue Snow would never have poisoned herself. Yet somehow she had swallowed cyanide. Suspicion soon fell on the Excedrin capsules. Might they have been tainted? They were sent for examination and the results clearly showed the presence of cyanide.

On June 16, the Food and Drug Administration (FDA) published the lot number of the contaminated capsules, and the manufacturer,

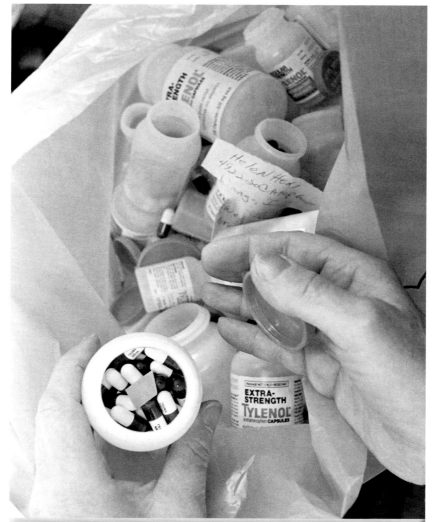

A Chicago city health department employee tests for cyanide in Tylenol capsules and tablets in October 1982. The city began testing after seven lives were claimed by cyanide-contaminated Tylenol. *AP Photo/Charlie Knoblock*

Bristol-Myers, cabled stores across the country to take all bottles of Extra Strength Excedrin off their shelves. During the sweep, Seattle police found two other bottles of cyanide-laced Excedrin, one in Auburn and the other in Kent, an adjoining suburb.

FBI CALLED IN

Because product tampering was now a federal offense, the FBI had assumed control of the investigation. Right from the outset they were stymied; like the Tylenol outrage, the crime seemed motiveless. No one called to claim responsibility for the attacks, nor was any financial demand made. And then, on June 17, one day after the widely publicized product recall, a 42-year-old widow named Stella Nickell telephoned the police with a strange story. Just 12 days earlier, she said, her husband Bruce, 52, had died suddenly after taking Extra Strength Excedrin capsules. She wondered if there could be any connection between his death and that of Sue Snow?

Although Bruce Nickell's autopsy had recorded the cause of death as emphysema and he had already been buried, an exhumation was unnecessary because the deceased had volunteered to be an organ donor. Consequently, a sample of his blood had been preserved. When that sample was tested, it too revealed the presence of cyanide. Even before the results were known, police officers had already recovered two bottles of suspect contaminated capsules from the Nickells' home.

An FBI chemist, Roger M. Martz, who had earlier examined the contaminated capsules found at the Snow residence, confirmed that the two Excedrin bottles from the Nickell home had been spiked. Another bottle of Excedrin recovered from a Kent supermarket was similarly contaminated, as was an Anacin bottle found at an Auburn store. The average amount of cyanide in the capsules was 700 milligrams, twice the lethal dose for an adult. Investigators now feared the worst: this was shaping up to be a rerun of the Chicago Tylenol outrage.

While agents struggled fruitlessly to establish some kind of connection between Bruce Nickell, a heavy equipment operator, and banker Sue Snow, a chemist at the FBI crime laboratory found something peculiar: all of the tainted capsules recovered so far contained particles of an algaecide used in home fish tanks. He even came up with the brand name—Algae Destroyer. Whoever spiked the capsules, it appeared, had mixed the cyanide in a container used previously to crush algaecide pellets.

Another, much more sinister, oddity emerged. During the course of the investigation, the FDA had examined more than 740,000 capsules sold throughout the Pacific Northwest and Alaska: yet only five bottles were contaminated, and of those bottles, two were found in Stella Nickell's home. Had she purchased both bottles at the same time, then it could have been ascribed to ill luck, but her claim to have bought them on different days and in different stores defied every known law of probability. The odds against such random misfortune were astronomical.

This anomaly immediately focused all investigative eyes on Stella Nickell. As a grandmother with two daughters, she seemed an unlikely killer. Also, neighbors said that she and Bruce had been happy together. It was the same at Seattle airport, where Stella worked as a security guard. Fellow employees described her as cheerful and hardworking: Bruce's death, they said, had devastated her, she had been inconsolable. But the FBI had found out something else—Stella Nickell had a fish tank in her home.

It might have been coincidence, of course, but combined with her improbable possession of two tainted bottles of Excedrin, this latest revelation catapulted Stella Nickell into the position of prime suspect. Agents visited local pet stores, anxious to know if anyone recalled a middle-aged woman buying Algae Destroyer. It was a long shot but on August 25 they got lucky. When shown a photo layout of various faces, a store clerk in Kent had no hesitation in identifying Nickell as having bought the algaecide from him. He remembered her distinctly because a little bell attached to her purse had jingled as she walked around the store.

As agents delved more deeply into her background, slowly the real Stella Nickell began to emerge. Between 1968 and 1971, while living in California, she had been convicted of check fraud, forgery and child abuse. Since then she had steered clear of the law but had not managed to steer clear of debt: the Nickells were permanently broke. At the time of Bruce's death, the bank was moving to foreclose on their home. Earlier, they had come perilously close to bankruptcy. And yet, despite this mountain of debt, in the past year Stella had somehow managed to find the money for extra insurance coverage on Bruce's life. As a state employee, he was already insured for $31,000, with an additional $105,000 should death result from an accident. Stella had topped up that sum with another $40,000 of coverage. In total, she stood to receive $176,000 if Bruce's death was judged to be accidental.

Except that the doctor who signed Bruce Nickell's death certificate had recorded emphysema as the cause, despite several phone calls

MURDER BY MAIL

Although random product tampering is a relatively recent phenomenon, the use of innocent-seeming products to mask evil intent is far from new. More than a century ago, in November 1898, Harry C. Barnet, a member of New York's swanky Knickerbocker Club, received an anonymous package by mail. It contained a bottle of Kutnow's Powder, a proprietary product that claimed to cure almost every ailment known to man. Barnet, who'd been feeling off-color for over a week, decided that he had nothing to lose and tried a dose. He was instantly sick. On November 10, Barnet succumbed to his illness. The certificate recorded the cause of death as "**cardiac asthenia**, caused by **diphtheria**."[2] One person greatly distressed by Barnet's death was his fiancée, Blanche Cheeseborough. However, Blanche wasn't the kind to let the grass grow under her feet. Nineteen days after Barnet breathed his last, his less than grieving ex-fiancée tripped down the aisle with Roland B. Molineux, a factory owner and another Knickerbocker Club member.

Just weeks later, only a cruel twist of fate prevented further inroads being made into the Knickerbocker's membership. Harry Cornish likewise received an anonymous package in the mail. It arrived on December 24 and contained a bottle of Bromo Seltzer. Cornish, who had no need of such a product himself, gladly permitted his housekeeper, Katherine J. Adams, to avail herself of the gift when she complained of a headache. After a single dose she collapsed, convulsing. Analysis of the Bromo Seltzer revealed the presence of mercury cyanide. It was quite obvious that the intended target had been Cornish. When document examiners were asked to compare the from an anxious-sounding Stella, frantic to learn if he could possibly have been mistaken in his findings. There was good reason for her concern. Under the provisions of the insurance policies, had Bruce Nickell died from cyanide during a product-tampering scare, then his

---

handwriting on the package with that of other club members, all agreed that it closely resembled that of Roland Molineux's. This was significant because, not too long previously, Cornish had bested Molineux in a weightlifting contest. Molineux had not taken his defeat well, and had accused Cornish of cheating. He was incensed enough to demand that the club's board expel Cornish. They had refused. Within a matter of days, Cornish had received his lethal package.

An exhumation of Barnet's body revealed that he, too, had been poisoned with cyanide. Upon receipt of this news, Kutnow Brothers, manufacturers of the tainted product, issued a $500 reward for information leading to the arrest of the perpetrator. By now most investigators were looking no further than Roland Molineux. He was sent for trial, but his claims of innocence and a defense backed by his father's wealth, failed to persuade 14 handwriting experts that the writing on both packages was other than his. Really damning evidence, however, came with the discovery that he had recently ordered a consignment of mercury cyanide, ostensibly for use in his factory. On February 19, 1900, Molineux was found guilty and sentenced to death. His family launched a lengthy appeal process. During his 18 months' stay in Sing Sing, Molineux wrote a book entitled *The Room with the Little Door*,[3] about his experiences on death row.

A second trial was granted in 1902, and the delay was to his advantage. Molineux posed as the victim of prejudice, won the verdict, and was set free. He wrote for several newspapers but lost heart after Blanche took off with another man and divorced him. His final years were spent in a slow decline. In 1913 his mind gave way completely and he entered New York State Hospital on Long Island. He died there on November 2, 1917.

death would have been ruled accidental and Stella would have pock-
eted the entire $176,000.

On November 18, more than five months after Sue Snow's death,
Nickell was brought in for questioning. She first denied ever buying
Algae Destroyer, then scoffed at suggestions that she had purchased
additional insurance on her husband's life. This second denial—so fool-
ish and unnecessary—immediately branded her as a liar. As the questions became more penetrating she brought the interview to a tearful
conclusion, angrily refusing to submit to a polygraph test. Inexplicably,
four days later she changed her mind. When asked by the examiner if
she had laced the capsules with cyanide, she replied no. The polygraph
needle jumped wildly. So did Nickell. Furious at the outcome, she
refused to say another word without benefit of counsel.

For several more weeks the case languished. Then, Stella's daughter,
Cindy Hamilton, 27, contacted the police. Although estranged from
her mother, she had felt an understandable loyalty when initially interviewed; now she wanted to clear her conscience. Her mother, she said,
had often talked of killing Bruce, even the possibility of hiring a hit
man. At other times, she had mentioned cyanide and had talked about
copying the Tylenol poisonings in Chicago. They, she said, "would be
very easy to reenact."[4]

Although convinced that Cindy was speaking the truth, prosecutors
knew that any competent defense lawyer would portray her testimony
as the product of a disaffected daughter out to gain revenge on the
mother she hated. It was while they pondered how best to combat this
likelihood that Cindy herself provided the answer. She mentioned that
her mother had researched the effects of cyanide at various libraries.
Immediately, agents began scouring every local library. In her home-
town of Auburn, an overdue notice came to light for a book that Stella
Nickell had borrowed and never returned, entitled *Human Poisoning*.[5]
Armed with her card number, an agent searched the aisles for every
book that Stella had borrowed. Inside a volume on toxic plants called
Deadly Harvest,[6] he found her number stamped twice on the checkout
slip—in 1983 and 1984, both dates before Bruce's death. Acting on a
hunch, he sent the book to the FBI crime laboratory.

PRINTS ON THE PAGES

There, fingerprint specialist Carl E. Collins examined every square inch of the book. He found no fewer than 84 of Nickell's prints on 47 different pages of *Deadly Harvest*, mostly from the section dealing with cyanide. He also found her prints in three encyclopedia volumes that dealt with poison. Altogether she had checked out five library books that discussed cyanide and other poisons.

Eventually, federal prosecutors decided that they had enough evidence to win an indictment against Stella Nickell. The courts agreed. On December 9, 1987, she was arraigned on five counts of murder and product tampering. Her trial began on April 20, 1988, when she became the first person in the nation charged with causing death by product tampering. Prosecutors painted a damning portrait of a psychopath prepared to use a product tampering panic to mask the murder of her husband, in order that she might profit from his death. Much of the most negative testimony came from the defendant's own daughter. "I know my mother very well, and basically, I knew she was capable of it," Cindy Hamilton sobbed on the witness stand. "But I was hoping she wouldn't."[7] With tears streaming down her face, Hamilton said she didn't warn her stepfather because she didn't think he would believe her. When the defense attacked Hamilton as someone lured into lying by the promise of a big payday (she eventually received a $250,000 reward from a drugs company), the prosecution countered by putting Kathy Parker on the stand. Parker, a Tacoma resident and a longtime friend of Hamilton's, testified that Hamilton told her of Nickell's plans in November 1985, more than seven months before Bruce died. "Cindy came home [and said], 'Katy, do you know what my mother just said to me? She asked me how much cocaine it would take to kill a person.'" Parker continued, "She (Hamilton) said that her mother had been talking about getting rid of her father … she was getting tired of him," Parker said.[8]

Stella Nickell decided to testify on her own behalf. But she fared poorly on her denials that she was tired of Bruce, when tackled by Assistant U.S. Attorney Joanne Maida. Nickell squirmed when Maida produced a letter, written to a bank on April 24, in which Nickell blamed her financial tribulations on "marriage problems"[9] that would soon be solved. She was also forced to admit that she and her husband owed various banks and an investment company $8,553 in May 1986. Ominously, just five days before Bruce's death, she wrote to the same bank, saying that "my payments will now stay current."[10]

On May 4, 1988, the case went to the jury. Their deliberations proved unusually tortuous. From the outset one juror held out for acquittal. District Judge William Dwyer, desperate to avoid the time and expense of a retrial, urged them to achieve unanimity. Then something strange happened. The holdout juror received an anonymous phone call. The caller

SUPERGLUE AND SUPER CLUES

Scientists are always looking to improve ways of lifting fingerprints from difficult surfaces. One of the most novel occurred in Winnipeg, Canada, after Shirley Andronovich, 42, had been found battered to death on May 19, 1990. The blood-drenched murder weapon lay beside her—a 55-pound slab of concrete. After a bizarre interlude in which Shirley's husband—an alcoholic who suffered blackouts—falsely confessed to the killing, detectives turned their attention to the murder weapon. Geologist Richard Munroe was asked if he could determine the source of the concrete slab. He returned to the crime scene at midnight in an attempt to reconstruct the chain of events. Standing in the deep shadows where the body was found, his attention was drawn to an illuminated area about 500 feet away. Moving closer, he saw two pieces of concrete, both superficially similar to the murder weapon.

Concrete is made by pouring sand, cement, water and aggregates into a mold. As it dries, the mixture assumes a distinctive pattern unique to that particular concrete block. Munroe used petrographic analysis to positively match the minerals in the murder weapon and the two pieces of concrete, then he took all three pieces and slotted them together like a jigsaw puzzle.

allegedly said, "Don't you all know that she [Nickell] failed the lie detector test?"[11] That fact had been withheld from the jury during the trial. (It was rumored that another juror had arranged for the call to be made.) When the juror, quite properly, told Judge Dwyer of the call, he asked if it would affect her decision. She said no. Despite defense demands for a mistrial, Judge Dwyer refused and deliberations were resumed.

After five days of often-contentious debate, on May 9 the jury convicted Nickell of murder. Following conviction, Dwyer again denied defense claims for a new trial, and instead sentenced Nickell to a prison term of 90 years.

Munroe now had an idea: What if the block held the killer's fingerprints? Obtaining prints from porous surfaces is fiendishly difficult, and Munroe decided to use the cyanoacrylate—or Superglue—method. This works by heating the sample in a small chamber, with a blob of Superglue, for around six hours. The fumes given off adhere to biological material such as the oil in fingerprints. Under a laser, this biological material fluoresces, producing a clear image of print. Unfortunately, the cyanoacrylate was the same color as the concrete. Munroe knew the prints were there, he just couldn't see them.

What he needed was a chemical that would attach itself to the cynoacrylate. After numerous fruitless attempts, he found a biological stain called Sudan Black that produced smudged but discernible prints.

Unfortunately the prints did not match any in the police database, and it wasn't until the Winnipeg media ran one-year anniversary stories on the case, that a major breakthrough came. An informant told police that on the night of the crime his roommate, Mark Jarman, a 29-year-old unemployed construction worker, had come in wearing bloodstained jeans and boots. The next day he'd burnt his clothes.

Once in custody, Jarman had his prints taken. They matched those found on the concrete block. He was eventually sentenced to life imprisonment.

A U.S. Marshal leads Stella Nickell from a federal courthouse in May 1988. Nickell was convicted of causing the deaths of her husband and Sue Snow by lacing Extra-Strength Excedrin with cyanide. *AP Photo/Gary Stewart*

Stella Nickell has no shortage of supporters who believe her to be innocent. Some claim to have new evidence. Others argue that the prosecution case was tainted, with accusations that Cindy Hamilton's testimony had been driven by a craving for the reward money. In 2001 Nickell herself appeared on the TV program *48 Hours*, defiant as always. She said, "I am not guilty. I did not kill my husband. And I won't quit fighting until I prove it."[12] Thus far she has failed in that endeavor. Her arguments and those of her supporters have fallen on barren ground. In

2001 a court decided that there was insufficient new evidence to grant a new trial.

At one time most crimes were solved by processing fairly limited amounts of evidence, and many still are. What the Tylenol tragedy and Stella Nickell's heartless crimes demonstrated was that the rules had shifted. Instead of scrutinizing a single crime scene, the investigator now needed to comb an area that extended for hundreds of square miles. And during the course of that investigation, items of evidence were uncovered that numbered in the millions. Even so, it was still old-fashioned greed that doomed Stella Nickell. Had she been content with $31,000, in all probability she would have escaped scot-free. Her craving for that extra $141,000 ruined what would have been the perfect crime.

The Evidence
Never Lies

American criminalist and blood spatter expert Herb Leon MacDonell wrote in 1984: *"In the course of a trial, defense and prosecuting attorneys may lie, witnesses may lie, the defendant may certainly lie. Even the judge may lie. Only the evidence never lies!"*[1]

Since that time, MacDonell's aphorism has been repeated so often that it is in danger of becoming a cliché, but it remains, nonetheless, *the* definitive statement on qualitative evidence analysis. As high-profile crimes turn into trials, and attorneys start spinning the story to suit their case, it is all too easy for the evidence to get pushed into the background. Suddenly, personalities begin to take center stage. This is especially true if the defendant is perceived as someone deserving of public sympathy. For instance, mothers are not supposed to kill their children. And yet many have done so. But some members of the general public will always rebel against such a possibility, echoing the 1909 closing argument of an English defense lawyer who thundered to the jury that such a charge was "morally incompatible with motherhood."[2] (It worked; the defendant, Florence Haskell, was acquitted, having almost certainly slashed the throat of her 10-year-old son.) Much the same sort of defense was offered in a Texas courtroom in 1997 when a young mother was accused of a remarkably similar crime. On this occasion, though, objectivity held sway. So far as the prosecution was concerned, strip out the overheated emotion, concentrate only on the evidence, and it is quite surprising how even complex tragedies fall into focus.

To most onlookers, Darlie and Darin Routier embodied the American dream. Still in their 20s, they had three great sons, owned a fine house in the swanky suburb of Rowlett, just outside Dallas, Texas and drove a Jaguar sports car, while Darin's thriving business—his company repaired mainframe computers—had netted him $100,000 in 1995. Then, in a few short minutes on June 6, 1996, the dream turned into the worst nightmare imaginable.

At some time after 2:00 A.M., an intruder broke into the house at 5801 Eagle Drive and crept into the living room where Darlie and her two eldest boys, Devon, age 6, and Damon, a year younger, lay fast asleep after watching TV. (Darlie had taken to sleeping downstairs because she was easily awoken by her six-month-old son, Drake, who was upstairs with his father.) The first Darlie knew of this break in was when she felt a knife at her throat and the presence of a man. Instinctively, she began fighting for her life.

After twice stabbing Darlie, the intruder ran off through the kitchen. Only then did Darlie realize that Devon and Damon had also been attacked. Both lay sprawled on the sofa, bleeding heavily. Dragging her shattered senses together, Darlie managed to dial 911. The time was 2:31 A.M. She was hysterical, screaming, "My babies are dying. They're dead. Oh my God."[3] Then the call took a strange turn. She suddenly told the dispatcher about a butcher knife that lay in the kitchen, adding apologetically, "I already picked it up," adding later, "God, I bet if we could have gotten the prints, maybe . . ."[4]

Arriving police officers walked into a scene of appalling carnage. Both boys had received deep, lethal stab wounds. Damon was alive, but barely; Devon was already dead. Darlie's own wounds, by contrast, were of the slicing type and far less severe, although one cut had gone perilously close to the carotid artery and would later require surgery. She described her assailant as a white male, about six feet tall, dressed all in black, black shirt, black jeans, and a black baseball cap. Surprisingly for such a light sleeper, she had not awoken during the murderous assault on her two sons, despite being on the same sofa. Asked later, how she had managed such an improbable feat, she had stammered, "I don't know how to answer that."[5]

While Darlie was taken to the hospital for medical attention—paramedics noticed that during the ambulance ride, not once did she inquire about the condition of her two sons (by this time Damon had also died)—investigators began moving through the house, trying to gain some sense of what had happened. A slashed window screen in the garage signified the intruder's apparent entry point. But the netting showed no sign of having been forced in or out to allow passage of a

IS IT HUMAN BLOOD?

Blood is, arguably, the most informative type of evidence there is. It is extremely durable and devilishly difficult to get rid of and through the modern miracle of DNA typing, a single speck of blood can be a certain indicator of identity. And that's not all. The patterns that blood makes as it exits a body can provide the experienced investigator with very strong clues as to how a crime was committed. But all these are recent innovations. Indeed, barely more than a century ago blood was impossible to even identify. Never was this more maddeningly demonstrated than when Ludwig Tessnow, a carpenter, was arrested in July 1901 on suspicion of having murdered two young brothers on the German island of Rugen. Tessnow protested that the dark stains on his work clothes came from various wood dyes that he used. And there was nothing to say otherwise. What really rubbed salt into the wound was the fact that, only three years previously, Tessnow had rolled out the same excuse when he was pulled in for questioning after the murder of two young girls. Then, as now, his explanation had frustrated the investigators who felt powerless to stop what they feared was a serial killer. But all that was about to change.

As the examining magistrate teetered on the verge of reluctantly freeing Tessnow, a newspaper item caught his eye. It told how a young biologist named Paul Uhlenhuth, at the nearby University of Greifswald, had recently developed a revolutionary new technique that could not only differentiate between blood and other stains, but also between human blood and the blood of other animals. Uhlenhuth, refining the body. Besides, any sensible burglar would have simply lifted the easily removable screen out of its frame. Also, the soft, dewy ground beneath the window showed no traces of any footprints or disturbance. In a nearby alley, a sock was found, possibly dropped by the assailant as he fled. While detectives waited for the K9 unit to arrive, they studied the

work of earlier scientists, had found that by injecting protein from a chicken's egg into rabbits, then mixing the rabbit serum with egg white, the egg proteins separated from the clear liquid to form a cloudy substance or *precipitate*. An extension of this process led to the production of rabbit-based serums that would precipitate, and therefore identify, the proteins of the blood of any animal, including humans.

The magistrate got in touch with Uhlenhuth, who agreed to examine a heavily stained pair of overalls taken from Tessnow's house, together with other items of clothing. After almost a week of painstaking study, on August 8, 1901, Uhlenhuth submitted his report. It was a report that would change the course of criminological history. As the prisoner had claimed, his overalls were indeed stained with wood dye, but Uhlenhuth also found 17 traces of what was undeniably human blood. Tessnow's suit and shirt yielded similar results; while his jacket, by contrast, was found to be contaminated with sheep's blood. After his trial and a lengthy confinement, Tessnow was executed at Greifswald Prison in 1904.

Nowadays Uhlenhuth's precipitin test, as it is known, has been greatly simplified. A liquid sample of suspected human blood is placed on a gelatin-treated glass slide next to a similar sample of the biological reagent. When an electric current is passed through the glass by means of electrodes, the protein molecules in the two samples filter outward through the gelatin toward each other. If a precipitin line forms where the antigens and the antibodies meet, this denotes that the sample is human blood. The precipitin test is extremely sensitive, requiring only minute samples. Positive results have been obtained on human blood that has been dried for a long as 15 years.

scene thoughtfully. The crime seemed motiveless. In the kitchen, neatly laid out on a countertop, lay a woman's purse and a display of expensive jewelry. Yet this had been ignored by the assailant. So what was his purpose in breaking into the house? And why kill two young children and let the only witness live? It didn't make sense.

The anomalies started coming thick and fast. In a frenzied attack, such as that inflicted on the Routier boys, the killer would have been drenched in blood, and yet there wasn't a trace of any blood outside the house along the murderer's apparent escape route. The only blood was found inside the house.

Nor did the living room exhibit many signs of having staged a life-or-death struggle. A lampshade was askew and a flower arrangement had been tipped over, and that was it. Even the flower stems were intact, as if the arrangement had been placed on its side rather than knocked asunder.

Darin Routier, who had been upstairs asleep with Drake at the time of the attack, had heard nothing. Neither had the family's dog—a yappy white Pomeranian that snapped continually at the heels of investigators as they carried out their duties—barked at any time during the break in. Something about this break in just didn't smell right.

DOGS LOSE THE SCENT

When the K9 unit arrived and the dogs were set loose, another problem surfaced. Bloodhounds have an extraordinary sense of smell, estimated to be hundreds of times more acute than that of humans, yet these dogs were unable to track the scent beyond where the sock was dropped. So either the killer had vaporized, or he had backtracked to the house.

More holes were beginning to appear in Darlie's story. She claimed to have chased the intruder through the kitchen, where he had knocked a wine glass on the floor. Yet the glass fragments were found *on top* of the blood drops, indicating that the glass had been dropped after—not before or during—the violence. Somehow, Darlie's bare feet had managed to miraculously negotiate this carpet of broken glass without sustaining a single cut.

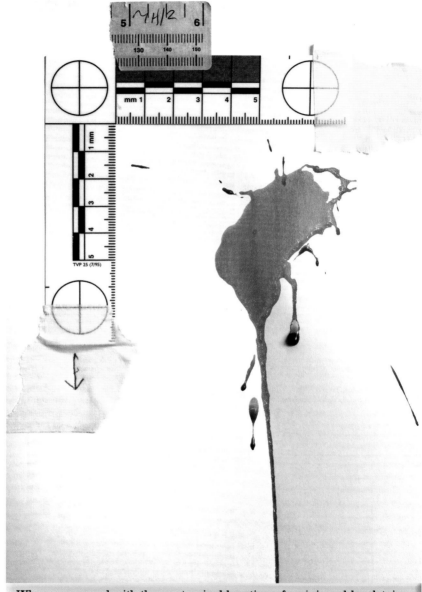

When compared with the anatomical location of an injury, bloodstains may provide information about the victim's position when the injury was inflicted and any subsequent movement of the injured party. Blood spatter analysis proved crucial in poking holes in Darlie Routier's fabricated story. *Jim Varney/Photo Researchers, Inc.*

She also said the assailant dropped the murder weapon—a 10-inch kitchen knife—by the door, before fleeing through the garage. She'd then picked up the knife and placed it on a counter. This accounted for her fingerprints on the knife. But blood spatter expert Tom Bevel could find no evidence to support the claim that the knife had been dropped on the kitchen floor. And, although Darlie's blood was found on a vacuum cleaner that had toppled over, the spatter wasn't consistent with someone running past, as she'd claimed. All the spots were circular, which meant they were deposited by someone either standing still or walking very slowly. Running produces a different pattern of blood spots, more elliptical in shape, usually with a tail indicating the path of the person. Bevel also found discrepancies in the blood pattern on Darlie's nightshirt, which she had been wearing at the time of the attack.

THE SOUNDS OF VIOLENCE

The analysis of sound is an emerging field in forensic science. It takes two main forms; forensic acoustics and forensic phonetics. Forensic Acoustics—the discipline that trapped Darlie Routier—deals with three main areas. These are:

1. Audio Enhancement: Where recordings are of poor quality, filters may be applied in an attempt to improve the intelligibility of a recording.
2. Recording Authentication: Various auditory, acoustic and other techniques are used to determine whether a recording has been edited or otherwise manipulated.
3. Miscellaneous: This deals with types of recorded materials other than speech. These might include gunfire, such as was analyzed on recordings of the assassination of President John F. Kennedy in 1963.

Forensic Phonetics deals mainly with the human voice and concentrates on four main areas. These are:

1. Voice Comparison: The analysis of two recorded speech samples. One sample is the speech of an unknown

The blood from her two sons had been sprayed onto the nightshirt, rather than smudged or wiped. Such a pattern would typically occur from the "fly off" from a knife or some other weapon, as it was wielded up and down in a stabbing or slicing motion.

With the investigation narrowing its focus at every turn, investigators recalled that when Darlie was first interviewed, she was holding a wet towel to her neck wound. Was it possible she had used this to clean up the house before they arrived? To find out, they used a spray called **luminol**. Luminol is a compound that luminesces when it comes into contact with blood—even traces that are years old. It is so sensitive, it can detect blood at 1 part per million, even after a cleanup has occurred.

Investigators began in the kitchen. They had noticed that the sink looked spotless, while the adjoining kitchen countertops were smudged,

---

perpetrator; the other sample is the speech of a suspect. An analyzer, sometimes aided by a computer program, attempts to evaluate the degree of consistency between the samples and, where consistent, the degree of distinctiveness of the samples.

2. Speaker Profiling: Where there is a recording of a criminal's speech but no suspect has been identified, a profile can be compiled of the speaker based on his or her speech patterns. Sophisticated analysis of regional accents and dialects can sometimes pinpoint, to within a few square miles, where the criminal was born/grew up.

3. Content Determination: This involves analysis of a recording where the content is uncertain, due to factors such as background noise or poor recording quality. By using various filters, the expert is able to isolate the desired content.

4. Voice Line-ups: Where a witness has heard a perpetrator's voice but has not seen his or her face, it is possible to construct a line-up of voice recordings that will form an auditory version of a conventional ID parade.

as though someone had made the effort to clean the sink of blood. They sprayed all the surfaces with luminol. With the kitchen light turned off, a bloody footprint glowed bluish-green in front of the sink. Beneath the sink, more blood was found, suggesting someone had stood still while bleeding. DNA tests confirmed all the blood to be Darlie's. It was the same with all the bloody footprints in the kitchen—every one belonged to Darlie.

So far as the experienced investigators were concerned, nothing in the house indicated the presence of an intruder.

If the blood raised doubts, then it was the taped 911 call that made a liar out of Darlie Routier. She had always insisted that she had phoned from the kitchen, and didn't enter either the living room or garage. But Barry Dickey, a forensic audio expert, knew differently. Sound is either absorbed or reflected by the various elements in a room; generally, soft surfaces tend to soak up sound, while hard surfaces such as glass and stone bounce the sound around. By eliminating all background noise, Dickey was able to isolate Darlie's voice, the varying wavelengths of which told him that the call had come from at least three different rooms. Detectives reasoned that, as she sobbed out her 911 story, Darlie had dashed from room to room, wiping away, or so she thought, the evidence of her misdeeds.

The clinching evidence came with the discovery of a minute glass fiber rod and some rubber dust on a bread knife found in the kitchen. When examined microscopically, the cut screen in the garage was found to be made from PVC bundles, the interior core of which was composed of glass fiber rods identical to that found on the knife. And the rubber dust was also consistent with having come from the cut PVC screen. This meant that whoever slashed the screen had already been inside the house.

With the evidence stacking up ominously against Darlie Routier, investigators were still baffled as to why an apparently successful wife and mother should suddenly snap and murder two of her children. One possible reason was uncovered at the hospital. When Darlie arrived, blood tests revealed the presence of amphetamines in her system. (After her most recent pregnancy she had been depressed over not losing lose weight and had begun taking pills to suppress her appetite.) But amphetamines can cause dangerous mood swings, and there were hints that she was already deeply afflicted by postpartum depression. The arrival of a third son had affected her badly; she had, reportedly, been desperate to have a daughter. Gradually her mood darkened. A diary that Darlie kept revealed her suicidal state of mind in the days preceding the attack.

KILLING FOR CASH?

Prosecutors also uncovered another, possibly more direct motive: money. The Routiers were in deep financial trouble. They were behind in their mortgage, the IRS was hounding them for unpaid back taxes, and, just days before the killings, they had been turned down for a $5,000 loan. (Coincidentally, each child had a $5,000 insurance policy on his life.)

On June 18 Darlie Routier was charged with double murder. When her trial began on January 6, 1997, prosecutors downplayed Darlie Routier's emotional problems and, instead, Dallas County assistant district attorney Greg Davis told the jury, "The evidence will show that the real Darlie Lynn Routier is a self-centered woman, a materialistic woman and a woman cold enough in fact to murder her own two children."[6] Frustrated by the possibility of losing her house, and the business, and being up to her eyes in debt, she blamed her children because she felt that "she was no longer the glamorous, blond center of attention."[7]

Time after time, the evidence was shown to conflict with Darlie Routier's story. Fingerprint expert Charles Hamilton told the jury that the only prints uncovered at the crime scene were those of Darlie and her children. Then, Charles Linch, an analyst for the Southwestern Institute of Forensic Sciences, testified that it was impossible for an intruder to have left the scene of the crime without leaving a trail of blood.

In response, all Darlie's five-strong defense team could offer was the argument that Darlie was simply not the type to murder her children. According to Greg Mulder, Darlie was a doting mother. "And the State wants you to believe she became a psychotic killer in the blink of an eye? . . . Well, folks, that's just absurd!"[8]

The jury thought otherwise. After just 10 hours of deliberation, on February 1, 1997, they convicted Darlie Routier of capital murder.

Darlie Routier is escorted into the Mountain View Correctional Facility in Gatesville, Texas, on February 5, 1997, after being sentenced to death for the murder of her two children. *AP Photo/ Ron Heflin*

Three days later she was sentenced to death. Despite numerous motions and appeals, she remains on death row at the Mountain View Correctional Facility.

As often happens in such high-profile cases, Darlie Routier has no shortage of supporters who believe her to be innocent of any involvement in the death of her two children. Web sites have sprung up, examining the circumstances of this tragedy in microscopic detail. Most are highly supportive of Darlie Routier. A common complaint is that she is a victim of "circumstantial evidence." Circumstantial evidence, however, is often the only evidence there is, and frequently the best evidence there is. In this case there were too many lies and too many glaring inconsistencies in Routier's account of events. Any other verdict would have flown in the face of common sense. For whatever reason—and it's possible that not even Darlie Routier herself can say why—in the early hours of June 6, 1996, this disturbed woman took a knife and butchered her two eldest sons. The evidence doesn't lie.

Endnotes

Introduction

1. The Innocence Project, "Know the Cases: James Tillman," http://www.innocenceproject.org/Content/272.php (Accessed October 14, 2009).
2. *Frye v. United States*, 293 F. 1013 (D.C. Cir. 1923).
3. Ibid.
4. *Daubert v. Merrell Dow Pharmaceuticals*, 509 U.S. 579 (1993).
5. Paul R Rice, *Evidence: Common Law and Federal Rules of Evidence* (Charlottesville, Va.: Lexis Law Publishing, 2000), 195.

Chapter 2

1. AP State & Local Wire, February 9, 2006.

Chapter 3

1. Cam Rossie, "Tape of '23 Minutes of Murder' To Be Introduced At Trial," AP, March 28, 1983
2. No Credit, UPI, April 14, 1993
3. Cam Rossie, "Prosecutors Play Tape Found on Body," AP, April 13, 1993.
4. "Jurors Hear Tape at Murder Trial," *New York Times*, April 14, 1983.
5. Cam Rossie, "Murder Defendant Testified He Acted Out of Desperation," AP, April 14, 1983.
6. Cam Rossie, "Psychiatrist Says Society Would Not Be Served by Locking Wolf Up," AP, April 15, 1983.
7. Cam Rossie, "Judge Calls Defendant's Court Testimony an 'Act,'" AP, April 19, 1983.
8. Cam Rossie, "Domestic News," AP, April 20, 1983.

Chapter 4

1. U.S. Department of Justice, "2007 Crime in the United States," http://www.fbi.gov/ucr/cius2007/offenses/expanded_information/data/shrtable_07.html (Accessed October 8, 2009).
2. David Willman, "Discord, Suspicions Mark Murder Case," *LA Times*, October 15, 1991.
3. Justine Kavanaugh-Brown, "Empty Disk Helps Convict Coffee-Can Murderer," Government Technology, http://www.govtech.com/gt/articles/96104 (Accessed October 9, 2009).
4. Ibid.
5. Elaine Woo, "Robert D. Chatterton, 66," *LA Times*, April 25, 2005.

6. Stuart Pfeifer, "Murder Defendant's Use of Poison Is Described," *Orange County Register*, April 6, 1995.

7. Jeff Collins, "Expert Backs Prosecution's Poison Theory," *Orange County Register,* June 25, 1992.

Chapter 5

1. Ellies O'Hanlon, "Angry Andrea Takes on Poison Pen Tormentor," Independent News and Media, http://www.independent.ie/opinion/analysis/angry-andrea-takes-on-poison-pen-tormentor-1280037.html (Accessed October 9, 2009).

2. Donald W. Foster, "Ideas in American Policing," National Criminal Justice Reference Service, http://www.ncjrs.gov/App/Publications/abstract.aspx?ID=194249 (Accessed October 9, 2009).

3. Caleb Crain, "Donald Foster Uses High-Powered Computer Tests," Webb Sleuths, http://meltingpot.fortunecity.com/macau/674/foster/background.html (Accessed October 9, 2009).

4. Bill Montgomery, "FBI: Prints Link Moody to Bomb," *Atlanta Constitution*, June 15, 1991.

5. Ibid.

6. Kevin T. McGhee, "Mail-Bomb Murder Trial Opens," *USA Today*, June 5, 1991.

7. Ed Stych, "Bombs That Killed Judge, Lawyer Similar to 1972 Bomb," AP, June 18, 1991.

8. Bill Montgomery, "Moody Gets Maximum Sentence," *Atlanta Constitution*, August 21, 1991.

9. Bill Montgomery, "Bomb Parts Traced to Taiwan," *Atlanta Constitution*, June 19, 1991.

Chapter 6

1. Diane Priest, "Arlington Detective's Hunch Pays Off," *Washington Post*, October 13, 1988.

2. Andee Hochman, "Lawyer's Killer Sentenced," *Washington Post*, February 5, 1985.

3. John Mintz, "$150,000 Bail Set," *Washington Post*, February 15, 1984.

4. "To Abolish the Third Degree," *New York Times*, July 6, 1902.

5. Diane Priest, "Rapist-Slayer Given 2nd Death Sentence," *Washington Post,* November 5, 1988.

6. The Prime Minister's Prizes for Science, "1998 Australia Prize," Department of Innovation, Industry, Science and Research, https://grants.innovation.gov.au/SciencePrize/Pages/Doc.aspx?name=previous_winners/Aust1998Jeffreys.htm (Accessed October 9, 2009).

7. Diane Priest, "Arlington Detective's Hunch Pays Off," *Washington Post*, October 13, 1988.

Chapter 7

1. Paul Rubin, "The Eternal Flame," *Phoenix New Times*, Features, August 13, 1998.

2. Ibid.

3. Brent Whiting, "Daughter Kept Mom's Burial Secret," *Vancouver Sun*, May 9, 1995.

4. L. Wayne Hicks, "A Real Dead-End Career," *Denver Business Journal*, July 26, 1996.

5. "Man Convicted in 1966 Killing," *Washington Post*, April 21, 1995.

6. Tara Meyer, "Memory of Murder," *Houston Chronicle*, April 22, 1995.

7. Karen Sorensen, "Memory Key to Solving Murder Mystery," *Journal Star*, May 21, 1995.

Chapter 8

1. "Lewis Denies Tylenol Killings," UPI, June 15, 1984

2. *State v. Molineux*, 68 N.Y. 264; 61 N.E. 286; 1901 N.Y.

3. Roland Molineux, *The Room with the Little Door* (G.W. Dillingham Company, New York, 1903).

4. George Tibbetts, "Daughter Says Defendant Discussed Copying Fatal Tylenol Poisoning Case," *The Oregonian*, April 27, 1988.

5. Janet Giltrow, *Academic Reading* (Buffalo, N.Y.: Broadview Press, 1974), 24.

6. J. M. Kingsbury. *Deadly Harvest* (New York: Holt, 1972).

7. Katia Blackburn, "Defendant Denies Cyanide Killings," *The Oregonian*, April 28, 1988.

8. Katia Blackburn, "Witness Supports Account of Murder Plot," *The Oregonian*, April 29, 1988.

9. Ibid.

10. Ibid.

11. George Tibbits, "Cyanide Slayer Found Guilty," *The Oregonian*, May 10, 1988.

12. 48 Hours, "Bitter Pill: A Wife on Trial," CBSNews.com, http://www.cbsnews.com/ stories/2001/06/04/48hours/ main294700.shtml (Posted July 25, 2002).

Chapter 9

1. Alfred Allan Lewis, and Herb Leon MacDonell, *The Evidence Never Lies* (New York: Holt, Rinehart & Winston, 1984), xiii.

2. Colin Evans, *The Father of Forensics* (New York: Berkley Books, 2007), 24.

3. John W. Gonzalez, "Routier Jury Told of Drugs," *Houston Chronicle*, January 9, 1997.

4. Ibid.

5. John W. Gonzalez, "Routier Takes Stand, Denies Killing Her Sons," *Houston Chronicle*, January 30, 1997.

6. Kelly Shannon, "Mother Accused of Killing Two Sons Goes on Trial," AP, January 6, 1997

7. Ibid.

8. Joseph Geringer, "Darlie Routier: Doting Mother/Deadly Mother," Tru TV Crime Library, http:// www.trutv.com/library/crime/ notorious_murders/women/ routier/1.html (Accessed October 14, 2009).

Glossary

anthropology   The study of mankind in general

ballistics   A widely used term for firearms and bullets analysis. Technically, it refers to the study of projectiles

bertillonage   A system of identification based on bodily measurements popular in the late 19th century; named after its founder, Alphonse Bertillon, it was superseded by the advent of fingerprinting

botany   The scientific study of plants and flowers

cardiac asthenia   An irregularity in the heart's functioning

chromatograph   An instrument that can analyze a sample and display its various component parts

cyanide   A highly toxic poison

dendrochronology   The science of dating the age of trees by studying the tree ring growth patterns

diphtheria   An infectious disease that affects the nose and throat. Now exceptionally rare in the United States

DNA   A common acronym for deoxyribonucleic acid; a nucleic acid that contains the genetic instructions used in the development and functioning of all known living organisms

entomology   The scientific study of insects

Freemasonry   A fraternal organization with an estimated worldwide membership of 5 million

geophysics   The scientific study of the earth's physical properties

inceptive evidence   Evidence that might open up other avenues of inquiry

luminol   A chemical that reacts with the iron in hemoglobin and gives off a distinctive blue glow; used to detect the presence of blood at crime scenes

microscopy   An all-encompassing term that covers the use of a microscope to study samples or objects

Miranda rights   A warning read out to a suspect at the time of arrest, advising that person of his or her constitutional rights

nitroglycerine   A volatile high explosive

prussic acid   Historical name for hydrogen cyanide

pyrotol   An explosive made from cordite and smokeless powder, available for a brief time shortly after World War I

recuse   To disqualify oneself as a judge in a particular case (usually to avoid a conflict of interest)

ricin   A rare and highly toxic poison cultivated from the castor bean

selenium   Naturally occurring metal that is toxic in high amounts

serology   The scientific study of blood

spectrograph   A scientific instrument that splits or disperses the light from an object into its component wavelengths so that it can be recorded and then analyzed

subcutaneous   Beneath the skin

toxicology   The study of poisons and their effects

waterboarding   A form of torture in which the victim is immobilized on his or her back with the head inclined downward, and then water is poured over the face and into the breathing passages

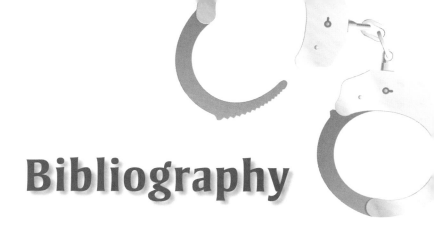

Bibliography

Baden, Michael, and Judith Adler Hennessee. *Unnatural Death*. London: Sphere, 1991.

Baldwin, James. *The Evidence of Things Not Seen*. New York: Holt, Rinehart & Winston, 1985.

Best, Arthur. *Evidence: Examples and Explanations*. New York: Aspen, 2007.

Block, Eugene. *The Wizard of Berkeley*. New York: Coward-McCann, 1958.

Cuthbert, C. R. M. *Science and the Detection of Crime*. London: Hutchinson, 1958.

Davis, Donald A. *Hush Little Babies.* New York: St. Martin's Paperbacks, 1997.

Di Maio, Vincent J. M. *Gunshot Wounds: Practical Aspects of Firearms, Ballistics, and Forensic Techniques*. New York: Elsevier Science Publishing Co., 1985.

Dower, Alan. *Crime Scientist*. London: John Long, 1965.

Emanuel, Steven. *Evidence*. New York: Aspen, 2004.

Evans, Colin. *The Casebook of Forensic Detection*. New York: Berkley, 2007.

Gaute, J. H. H., and Robin Odell. *Murder 'Whatdunit'*. London: Harrap, 1982.

Gaute, J. H. H., and Robin Odell. *The New Murderers' Who's Who*. New York: Dorset Press, 1979.

Gerber Samuel (ed). *Chemistry and Crime: From Sherlock Holmes to Today's Courtroom*. Washington, D.C.: American Chemical Society, 1983.

Houts, Marshall. *Where Death Delights*. New York: Coward-McCann, 1967.

Innes, Brian. *Bodies of Evidence*. Leicester, UK: Silverdale, 2000.

Jenkins, Ray. *Blind Vengeance*. Athens, Ga.: University of Georgia Press, 1997.

Knapmann, Edward W. (ed.) *Great American Trials*. Detroit: Visible Ink, 1994.

Lane, Brian. *Encyclopedia of Forensic Science*. London: Headline, 1992.

Lassiter, G. Daniel (ed). *Interrogations, Confessions, and Entrapment*. New York: Kluwer Academic, 2004.

Lee, Henry C., Timothy Palmbach, and Marilyn T. Miller. *Henry Lee's Crime Scene Handbook*. London: Academic, 2001.

Lewis, Alfred Allan, and Herb MacDonell. *The Evidence Never Lies*. New York: Holt, Rinehart & Winston, 1984.

Marriner, Brian. *Forensic Clues to Murder*. London: Arrow, 1991.

McAdams, Frank, and Tim Carney. *Final Affair*. New York: Berkley, 2002.

Morland, Nigel. *Science in Crime Detection*. London: Hale, 1958.

Odell, Robin. *Science Against Crime*. London: Marshall Cavendish, 1982.

Olsen, Gregg. *Bitter Almonds*. New York: Warner Books, 1995.

Rice, Paul R. *Evidence: Common Law and Federal Rules of Evidence.* Charlottesville, Va.: Lexis Law Publishing, 2000.

Saferstein, Richard. *Criminalistics: an Introduction to Forensic Science.* Upper Saddle River, N.J.: Prentice Hall, 1998.

Smyth, Frank. *Cause of Death.* London: Pan Books, 1982.

Stevens, Serita, and Anne Bannon. *HowDunit—The Book of Poisons.* Cincinnati: Writer's Digest Books, 2007.

Thompson, John. *Crime Scientist.* London: Harrap & Co., 1980.

Thorwald, Jürgen. *The Century of the Detective.* New York: Harcourt, Brace & World, 1965.

Timbrell, John. *Introduction to Toxicology.* New York: Taylor & Francis, 2002.

Wecht, Cyril, Mark Curriden, and Benjamin Wecht. *Cause of Death.* New York: Dutton, 1993.

Wilson, Colin, and Patricia Pitman. *The Encyclopedia of Murder.* New York: Putnam's, 1962.

Wilson, Colin, and Donald Seaman. *The Encyclopedia of Modern Murder.* New York: Putnam's, 1983.

Wilson, Colin. *Written in Blood: A History of Forensic Detection.* New York: Carroll & Graf, 2003.

Wonder, Anita. *Bloodstain Pattern Evidence.* San Diego: Academic Press, 2007

Further Resources

Journals

Fischer, Mary A. "Was Wayne Williams Framed?" *Gentlemen's Quarterly* (April 1991): 228ff

Koltz, Charles. "The Atlanta Murders," *New Jersey Law Journal* (December 3, 1981): 11ff

Jackson, Donald Dale. "Who Killed Bruce Nickell and Sue Snow," *Reader's Digest* (February 1991), 149–154.

Court Cases

Commonwealth v. Nicola Sacco & another, 255 Mass. 369, 151 N.E. 839 (Mass. 1926).

Alabama v. Moody, 684 So. 2d 114 (1996).

United States v. Moody, 977 F.2d 1425 (11th Cir. 1992).

Spencer v. Commonwealth of Virginia, 238 Va. 275, 384 S.E.2d 775 (1989).

Spencer v. Commonwealth of Virginia, 238 Va. 295, 384 S.E.2d 785 (1989).

Spencer v. Commonwealth of Virginia, 238 Va. 563, 385 S.E.2d 850 (1989).

Routier vs. State, 541 U.S. 1040, 124 S. Ct. 2157, 158 L. Ed. 2d 728 (2004).

Web Sites

CBS News. "Bitter Pill: A Wife On Trial"
http://www.cbsnews.com/stories/2001/06/04/48hours/main294700.shtml

The Phoenix New Times. **"The Eternal Flame"**
http://www.phoenixnewtimes.com/1998-08-13/news/the-eternal-flame/1

The Innocence Project
http://www.innocenceproject.org/

The Polygraph Museum
http://www.lie2me.net/thepolygraphmuseum/id16.html

Index

About the Author

Colin Evans is the author of numerous articles and books that deal with the history and development of forensic science. He has written *Blood on the Table: The Greatest Cases of New York City's Office of the Chief Medical Examiner*, *The Casebook of Forensic Detection*, *Criminal Investigations: Crime Scene Investigation*, and *The Father of Forensics: The Groundbreaking Cases of Sir Bernard Spilsbury and the Beginnings of Modern CSI*, and others. He lives in the United Kingdom. To find out more, visit his Web site at http://www.colin-evansonline.com